How to Be a Husband

Tim Dowling

CENTER POINT LARGE PRINT
THORNDIKE, MAINE

To Sophie; who else?

This Center Point Large Print edition
is published in the year 2015 by arrangement with
Blue Rider Press, an imprint of Penguin Publishing Group, a
division of Penguin Random House LLC.

Copyright © 2014 by Tim Dowling.

The text of this Large Print edition is unabridged.
In other aspects, this book may vary from the original edition.
Printed in the United States of America on permanent paper.
Set in 16-point Times New Roman type.

ISBN: 978-1-62899-649-4

Library of Congress Cataloging-in-Publication Data

Dowling, Tim, 1963–
    How to be a husband / Tim Dowling. — Center Point Large Print
edition.
    pages cm
    Summary: "A riotously funny book about how to be a good husband
(not like he would know) by Tim Dowling, star columnist for *The
Guardian*. Think Nick Hornby meets Dave Barry—with a hint of
Modern Family"—Provided by publisher.
    ISBN 978-1-62899-649-4 (library binding : alk. paper)
    1. Husbands—Humor. 2. Marriage—Humor. 3. Large type books.
        I. Title.
    PN6231.H8D69 2015b
    818´.602—dc23
                                                        2015015445

Introduction

In the summer of 2007 I was asked out of the blue to take over the page at the front of the *Guardian*'s *Weekend* magazine. I say out of the blue, but I'll admit it was a possibility I'd considered long before the invitation was extended. I therefore received the news with my usual mixture of gratitude and impatience—shocked, thrilled, immensely flattered, and not before time. There was no question of turning down the offer, just tremendous apprehension at the idea of accepting. If I'd thought about wanting it a lot over the years, I hadn't really given much thought to doing it. What would my weekly column be about?

"I don't want you to feel you have to write about your own life," read the only e-mail I received from the editor on the subject. Perhaps, I thought, she doesn't want me to feel constrained by a particular format, or maybe she was wary because the only time I'd ever stood in for my predecessor, Jon Ronson, I'd written about an ordinary domestic event, and the magazine subsequently printed a letter that said, "May I suggest that the mystery smell in Tim Dowling's house is coming from his own backside as he emanates his natural air of smugness and pomposity?"

Whatever the reason, I felt I had my instructions: write about anything you like, except yourself.

The editor promptly took maternity leave, and I heard nothing more. The only additional information I received was a date for the first column, in mid-September. As the deadline approached I panicked, and wrote a piece about the dog and the cat following me around the house all day, precisely the sort of thing I'd been warned against. As I hit send I pictured myself having to defend it ("It's true! They do follow me!") at a hastily convened crisis meeting.

Nothing was said, and the column appeared as written. I wondered if the ban on domestic subjects had even been passed on. I decided it didn't matter, because now I had a full week to get my shit together.

The next column was a tightly wrought spoof apology taking in some recent scandals dogging the BBC, which had the twin advantages of being extremely topical and almost exactly the right length. Two weeks later, however, I suffered another failure of imagination, and at the last minute I wrote about my wife's amusingly callous reaction when I got knocked off my bike by a taxi. I wondered if it was possible to get sacked less than a month in.

Already I was beginning to feel the pressure of a weekly column; on the following deadline day I found myself in South America on another assignment, jet-lagged and bereft of inspiration. After a lot of hand-wringing and hair-pulling, I concocted a parody of those book group discussion questions you find at the back of paperback novels, based entirely on the only reading material I had with me.

A week later, in response to a report suggesting that Neanderthals may have possessed the power of speech, I cobbled together a hilarious dialogue between a Neanderthal couple who were expecting the *Homo sapiens* next door for supper. With more time I might have come up with a better ending, but as I read it over I felt I was finally starting to find my feet.

The panic returned soon enough. The upcoming Christmas deadlines required several columns to be done in advance. Over the next few weeks I wrote almost exclusively about domestic crises— arguments in front of the telly, arguments about the children, the window cleaner, even about the column itself. I filed each one with a sense of failure and a silent promise to myself that I would adhere more closely to the original brief the following week. When I finally managed to write something with a less personal, more sophisticated conceit, I received an e-mail from the editor, the first real feedback I'd had in months. It said, "What happened to the funny wife?"

And that is how I came splashing my marriage all over the papers. I never really had time to sit down and consider the ethical implications, if any. I know other people see writing about one's family as a pursuit full of interesting moral pitfalls, but I lacked the luxury of that perspective. In fact, a full six months elapsed before I actually realized what it was I was trying to achieve with my new column: I was trying to make my wife laugh.

She is almost the only person who reads what I write in front of me, and I have come to think of her as the planet's main arbiter of what is and isn't funny. Even as I was struggling to produce less personal, more abstract columns, I was noticing that she wasn't laughing at them. She read the Neanderthal one in complete silence in bed one Saturday morning, and then sighed and said, "I miss Jon Ronson."

But she was reliably amused by any column in which she was featured, often laughing out loud while reading back her own words.

"I'm funny," she would say, cackling. "You just write it down."

It is, of course, a delicate balancing act, requiring tact, sound judgment, and a good deal of empathy, which is why I have on several occasions got it badly wrong.

"I don't like when it says 'my wife' in the headline," said my wife one Saturday in early 2008. She had never before objected to my referring to her only as "my wife"—appreciating, I think, the halfhearted stab at preserving her anonymity—but spelled out in big letters, the term suddenly looked dismissive and belittling, especially in a headline like the one she was reading: "I don't like it when my wife hires people and then leaves their stewardship to me." It was an understandable objection, one that required a tactful, carefully worded response.

"I don't do the headline," I said. "They do the headline."

Some months later she told me I couldn't write about our eldest son referring to her as a "self-esteem roller," but it didn't feel like a gem I could relinquish easily. I wrote about it anyway, including her objection in the piece, and decided to treat her stony silence as tacit approval.

Six months after that my wife exclaimed, apropos of nothing, that she would divorce me if I ever wrote that I found her watching *Dog Borstal*. It seemed like a bluff worth calling.

One rainy day during our summer holiday in Cornwall, she looked up from the newspaper at me with very angry eyes.

"You've gone too far," she said. I looked back blankly—by the time the paper comes out, I don't always remember what I've written.

"What are you talking about?" I said.

"You compared me to the Canoe Wife!" she shouted. Then I remembered: we'd been bickering while watching something on the news about the Canoe Man—who had disappeared after rowing off in what was, I believe, technically a kayak—and his wife, who conspired with him to fake his death so they could start a new life in Panama.

"I think you're misreading it," I said. When I looked at it again later I could see where I might have inadvertently drawn some parallels between my wife and the Canoe Wife, but I still thought her interpretation required a pretty ungenerous assessment of my intent.

She spent the rest of the afternoon ringing people who she knew would agree that I had gone too far. Under the circumstances I did the only thing I could think of: I wrote about that too.

More than a year went by before it happened again: this time my wife was furious—properly furious—because I had written something she didn't like, in a column in which she barely appeared. Her explanation didn't make much sense to me (I won't risk attempting to reiterate it), but there was no mistaking her anger.

I realized that it didn't matter that I didn't get it, that her reaction was reason enough to stop doing the column if she wanted me to—she didn't even have to give me a week's notice. I briefly thought about offering to quit, until I weighed the chances that she might, in her current mood, take me up on it.

There were a couple of obvious solutions to the problem. I could have steered clear of writing about my marriage, although my wife insisted she was not uncomfortable with the column itself—she just got occasionally pissed off with an infelicitous phrase she thought might get her into trouble at work, although this only happened once, and neither of us saw it coming that time.

I could, I suppose, show her the column before-hand to give her a chance to voice specific objections, but I don't like her seeing it ahead of time, because then she might not laugh the next Saturday. It's meant to be a surprise.

To be honest, I wish I'd upset my wife with a callously worded phrase as few times in real life as I have done in my column. I do lots of stupid and unkind things in the course of my marriage, but with the column I get a whole week to figure out where I went wrong and, in effect, apologize.

An obligation to write about one's marriage carries the risk that one might be reduced to creating conflict simply in order to fulfill a weekly word count. The truth is, I've never had to. People may find this hard to believe, just as I find it difficult to imagine a marriage so well conducted that it lacks the disquiet required to sustain a weekly column. To be honest, I'm not sure I'd want to be part of a marriage like that, anyway. Chances are the couple in question wouldn't be that into it either.

Twenty years ago my wife and I embarked on a project so foolhardy, the prospect of which seemed to us both so weary, stale, and flat, that even thinking about it made us shudder. Neither of us actually proposed to the other, because neither of us could possibly make a case for the idea. We simply agreed—we'll get married—with the resigned determination of two people plotting to bury a body in the woods. Except that if you did agree to bury a body in the woods, you probably wouldn't ring your parents straightaway to tell them the news.

Two decades on we are still together, still married and still, well, if I hesitate to say "happy," it's only because it's one of those absolute terms, like "nit-free," that life has taught me to deploy with caution. It feels inherently risky to express contentment: I know that twenty years of marriage doesn't necessarily guarantee you ten more.

I can only really speak for myself, and while I would concede that I am on balance, content, there also isn't a day that goes by without my stopping to think: What the hell happened to you? Not, you know, in a bad way. But I'm still surprised, every day.

This is not really a self-help manual. If you come across anything that resembles advice in it, I would caution against following it too strictly, although I'm aware that is, in itself, advice. The kind of people who read self-help books are not, I'm guessing, looking to be more like me.

This is simply the story of how I ended up here,

and along with it an examination of what it means to be a husband in the twenty-first century, and what is and isn't required to hold that office these days. I can't pretend to offer much in the way of solid advice on how to be a man. Just as my sons think admonitions such as "Don't panic!" sound a bit rich coming from me, so would any tips I could possibly give about attaining manhood. I tried to become a man, but in the end I just got older.

But "husband"—it's one of the main things on my CV, right below "BA, English" and just above "Once got into a shark cage for money." "Husband" is the thing I do that makes everything else I do seem like a hobby.

Although I wear the distinction with pride, I'm aware that the title "husband" is not one that affords much respect these days. It was always a bit of an odd word. Of Old Norse derivation, "husband" basically means "master of a household," a sense that still lingers in the word "husbandry," referring to the stewardship of land and/or animals, and doesn't apply to me at all.

No other European language uses a word like "husband" to mean husband. In Sweden they say "man"; in Denmark, "mand." The French use the much more egalitarian "mari," which just means "married male," although it's easy to confuse with the girl's name "Marie," and also the French word for "mayor's office." As a consequence I often mistake the most basic French pleasantries for admissions of intrigue.

"Husband," on the other hand, sounds like an arcane office long shorn of its trappings, and is therefore faintly comical. It's like calling someone for whom you have no respect "chief." So while I feel able to use the word "wife" with a mixture of pride and delight ("Hey look! Here comes my wife!"), my wife only ever uses the phrase "Have you met my husband?" as a punch line, generally when she overhears people discussing the perils of self-Googling.

But, I hear you ask, are you a good husband? Ultimately that is for my wife alone to judge, but I think I know what she would say: no. Still, I can't help feeling there's a longer answer, a more considered, qualified way of saying no. If nothing else, I can look back and point out the detours round some of the pitfalls I was fortunate enough to overstep, and relate a few cautionary tales about the ones I fell headlong into.

When the well-off and the well-known retrace their path to success for the benefit of people seeking to follow their lead, the accounts tend to be colored by "survivorship bias"—they simply don't reckon with the examples of thousands of other people who followed a similar route and ended up nowhere. In hindsight, success can look like a repeatable formula composed of hard work and a series of canny decisions. No entrepreneur ever wrote a memoir that said, "Then I did something terribly risky and not all that clever, but once again fortune chose to reward my stupidity."

I don't have the luxury of revealing the secret of my success, even in hindsight. I didn't get where I am today—husband, father, gainfully employed person—by executing a deliberate strategy. I got where I am today by accident. One cold winter's evening twenty-four years ago, my life jumped its tracks without warning. As far as I'm concerned, all I did was hang on.

My successful marriage is built of mistakes. It may be founded on love, trust, and a shared sense of purpose, but it runs on a steady diet of cowardice, impatience, ill-advised remarks, and low cunning. But also: apologies, belated expressions of gratitude, and frequent appeals for calm. Every day is a lesson in what I'm doing wrong. Looking back over the course of twenty years it's obvious the only really smart thing I did was choose the right person in the first place, and I'm not certain I did that on purpose.

And even if I did choose wisely, I also had to be chosen. How often does that happen? This is what I'm saying: luck, pure and simple.

1.

The Beginning

It is a few days after Christmas, 1989. I am living in New York, working at a dead-end job. It's worse than that; I'm employed by the production department of a failing magazine. I probably won't even have my dead-end job for much longer.

I've just taken the train in from my parents' house in Connecticut. It's cold, and the city has an air of spent goodwill: there are already Christmas trees lying on the pavement. I drop by the apartment of some friends, two girls who share a grand duplex in the West Village. I know they have people visiting, English people. But when I get there my friend Pat—who is himself English but lives in New York—answers the door. He gives me to understand that the two roommates are in the basement having a protracted disagreement. They argue a lot, those two, and have a tendency toward high drama.

I first see the English girl as she comes up from downstairs, where she has been attempting, in vain, to broker some sort of truce and salvage the evening. Her short hair, charged with static, is riding up on itself at the back. She walks into the room, pauses to light a cigarette, and then looks at Pat and me.

"It's like a fucking Sartre play down there," she says.

We all go out to a bar. The English girl has a bright red coat and swears a lot. Her voice is husky, lower than mine. She is at once afraid of everything—she thinks she's going to be murdered on the streets of Greenwich Village—and nothing. She is funny and charming, but also peremptory and unpredictable, with shiny little raisin eyes.

"So," I say turning to her. "How long are you here for?"

"Look," she says, appraising me coolly. "It's almost as if we're having a conversation."

If I'm honest, she scares the shit out of me. But by the end of the evening I very badly want the English girl to be my girlfriend. My plan is to engineer this outcome as quickly as possible.

There are a few flaws in my plan: the English girl lives in London, and I live in New York; I already have a girlfriend of some four years' standing; the English girl does not appear to like me.

Nevertheless, at a New Year's Eve party a few days later, after several hours of the sort of unrelenting flirtation that might better be characterized as lobbying, I convince her to kiss me. She doesn't seem terribly flattered by my persistence, but I suppose a man who arranges to spend New Year's Eve apart from his actual girlfriend so he can try it on with a comparative stranger is, first and foremost, a heel. She has every reason to be circumspect.

I'm not normally this decisive, or resolute, or forward. A born torchbearer, I managed to keep my feelings completely hidden from the first three girls I fell in love with: Sarah, aged eight, who eventually moved away; Paula, aged ten, who also moved away; and Cati, aged eleven, who refused to do me the kindness of moving away. I'd come to understand love as an exquisite private pain by the time Jenni, aged fifteen, cornered me long enough to become my first girlfriend.

It's not that I'd never pursued anyone before; I just normally did it in a way that took the object of my affections a very long time to notice. I preferred to play it cool: waiting around in places where the girl I fancied might possibly turn up later, that sort of thing. This way I left myself an exit strategy whenever rejection presented itself —the paper trail of my courtship was nonexistent—although in most cases the girl in question simply found another boyfriend while my long game was still unfurling.

I don't have time for any of that now. I have just two weeks to break up with my girlfriend and convince the English girl that she should not only like me, she should take me back to England with her.

It is a difficult fortnight. The English girl's lacerating wit makes her a very hard person to have a crush on. We go out together several times, but we drink so much that I often have to reacquaint her with our relationship's forward progress the next morning. "You like me now," I tell her. "It's all been agreed."

I also discover I have rivals, including a guy who engineers sound systems for nightclubs and who, she tells me, has a gun in the glove box of his pickup truck. I can't compete with that. I don't have a gun, or a glove box to put it in.

I break up with my girlfriend one evening after work, in a bar called the Cowgirl Hall of Fame, an episode of shameful expediency I hope won't haunt me for the rest of my life, but it does a little. I have to ask for the bill while she's crying, because I have a date.

This is not how I usually break up with people: directly, implacably, while sitting on one hand to stop myself looking at my watch. In fact I don't have a usual method; I've never needed to develop a technique. Girls break up with me. That's what happened the last time, and the time before that, and the time before that.

After hailing a cab for my weeping ex-girlfriend, I walk to a bar—the same bar as that first night—where the English girl is waiting for me.

We are meeting here because our mutual friends do not approve of our burgeoning romance. They see me, not without cause, as an opportunist. The English girl has only recently come out of a long relationship—not quite as recently as eight minutes ago, mind—and it is generally acknowledged that I am being reckless with her affections. I only know that I'm being reckless with mine. In any case, I am currently unwelcome at the apartment where the English girl is staying.

So we meet at this bar most evenings. We drink martinis and laugh and then go back to my basement apartment, which is dark and generally grubby, except for my room, which is squalid. I leave her there in the mornings to go to work, and at some point during the day she comes and drops off my keys. Occasionally, for a change of pace, we meet at a different bar. Sometimes we go out with English friends of hers. They like to drink—a lot—and they don't seem very interested in eating.

One thing we have failed to do over the course of the fortnight is go on anything approaching a proper date. Finally, toward the end of her visit, we arrange dinner in a cozy and unhygienic restaurant in the Bowery. Our mutual friend Pat is our waiter. The hard living of the past two weeks, combined with full-time employment, has taken its toll on me. During the meal I begin to feel unwell. My stomach churns alarmingly and I break out in a cold sweat. I'm trying to be lively and charming, but I'm finding it hard to keep track of the conversation. I push the food around my plate. I manage a few glasses of wine, enough to realize what a terrible idea drinking is. Finally, the plates are cleared. I pay the bill. She offers to pay half, but I refuse. When I stand up from my chair, I feel something deep in my bowels give way with a lurch. I excuse myself and nip to the toilets, which are fortunately close at hand.

I do not wish to go into too much unpleasant detail. Suffice it to say I needed to spend about ten minutes in the loo to deal with the matter at hand, and found it necessary to part with my underpants forever. On lifting the lid of the wastebasket I discover that I am not the first customer to face that problem this evening. Even so, I decide to throw them out the window.

I come back to the table with all the nonchalance I can muster, but I know from looking in the toilet's scarred mirror how pale I am.

"Are you okay?" she says. "You were in there for a very long time."

"Yeah, fine," I say. Our mutual friend approaches, no longer wearing his waiter's apron.

"Pat's finished his shift," she says, "so we thought we'd all go next door for a drink."

"Oh," I say. "Okay."

I only need to drink two beers in a seedy bar to complete my charade of wellness, before our hugely successful first date comes to an end.

In the end the English girl flies back to London without me, but I have her phone number and her address. I write to her. I pick up a passport renewal application. Without telling anyone, I quietly lay plans to extricate myself from my own life.

How do I know the English girl is the one for me? I don't. And I certainly don't know if she thinks I am the one for her. Separated by an ocean, I begin to speculate about how I would feel if my holiday fling—an underwhelming American guy with a basement apartment and a dead-end job—kept ringing me to firm up what were supposed to be empty promises to visit. I would be distant and terse on the phone, I think —just like she is. I wonder if I am spoiling what we had by trying to prolong it.

Before I have even got my passport photo taken, she rings: she's found a cheap flight, she tells me, and is thinking about coming back for the weekend. It takes me a moment to process this news, which is slightly incompatible with her general lack of enthusiasm for our long-distance love affair. I know she hates flying. I can only conclude that she must like me more than she's been letting on. I'm a little stunned by the realization.

"Okay," I say.

"Try not to sound too fucking thrilled," she says.

When I catch sight of her at the airport I feel my face go bright red. I'm suddenly embarrassed by how little we know each other. Two weeks in each other's company, on and off, plus four phone calls and a letter apiece. We've had sex, like, eight times. We've been apart for a month. She doesn't even quite look the way I've remembered her. That's because I have no photo at home to consult.

There wasn't much time to prepare for her visit, but I have done one thing: I've bought a new bed. My old one was small, borrowed, and lumpy. The new one, delivered within twenty-four hours, touches three walls of my room. The bare mattress, silvery white, stands in sharp contrast to the grubby walls and the small, barred window that shows the ankles of passersby. At the age of twenty-six, it's probably the most expensive thing I've ever bought, and I'm embarrassed by it. I had only wished to provide an acceptable standard of accommodation, but it looks as if I've hired a sex trampoline for the weekend.

The next day she is woozy with jet lag. We stay in bed for most of the morning. At some point I sit up and see something on the floor that makes my heart sink: an uncompleted work assignment —a mock-up of a new table of contents page. It's been on my Things to Freak Out About list for weeks, and I've promised to deliver it by Monday. I pick it up and look it over. I've done no work at all on it, and now, clearly, I wasn't going to.

"What's that?" she says.

"Nothing. Something I'm supposed to have done."

"Let's have a look," she says.

"That's all dummy copy," I say. "I'm meant to write the words, but I don't know where to begin. To be honest, it's ruining my life."

"It can't be that difficult," she says. "You just need a stupid pun for each heading, and then a pithy summary underneath."

"It's a bit more complicated than that," I say.

"No, it isn't," she says. "Give me a pen." She does the first one, scribbling the words in the margin.

"That's not bad," I say.

"There you are," she says. "Only eleven more to go." She sits there with me, in my new bed, a fag hanging from her lips, treating my dreaded assignment like a crossword puzzle and completing it in under an hour. Two thoughts flash through my head simultaneously: Amazing! She can solve all my problems for me! and, Holy shit! She's smarter than I am!

Just before we finish my phone rings. It's my mother, who unbeknownst to me has driven into New York with my aunt to see some Broadway show. They are heading for a restaurant downtown, near me, and want to know what I'm doing for lunch. My heart starts to pound. I've never told my mother anything about the English girl who is smoking in my bed. I doubt she even knows I've broken up with my old girlfriend; she certainly didn't hear it from me. I sit in silence, phone to ear, for so long that the English girl raises an eyebrow.

"Can I bring someone?" I say finally.

It is the single most alarming dining experience I've ever endured, including the one that ended with my throwing my underpants out a toilet window. We have about fifteen minutes to get dressed and get there, and there is no time to brief the English girl on what to expect. The occasion is more formal than I'd anticipated: the restaurant, which I'd never heard of, is a bit grand, and my mother and my aunt are all dressed up. They have no idea who this girl from London is, or quite why I've brought her to lunch instead of, say, my girlfriend. I don't quite recognize the English girl myself: she has suddenly turned polite and circumspect, even a little demure. She doesn't swear once during the meal. I was surprised she's even agreed to come, but she's making a better fist of the occasion than I am. My brain keeps leaving my body to watch from the ceiling.

There is no point in the proceedings when I can draw my mother aside and explain why I've turned up to lunch with a mysterious English woman. Whenever they look at me both my aunt and my mother have legible question marks furrowed into their brows, but they are afraid to ask too much, having no idea where the answers might take the conversation. And we have prepared no lies. This, I realize too late, is a huge oversight.

The most anodyne inquiries ("So, how long are you in America for?") are met with unintentionally provocative responses ("Oh, not long. About thirty-six hours"). I'm trying to steer the conversation away from questions generally, especially the ones the English girl and I have never asked each other: What exactly is the nature of this relationship? But he lives here and you live there—how is that going to work?

By the time food arrives my mother and my aunt have begun to exchange meaningful glances. My biggest fear is that the English girl will go to the loo at some point, leaving me alone with them.

"That was weird," she says afterward, lighting a cigarette as we reach the safety of the corner.

"Sorry," I say. "But it's good you've finally met my mother. Now we can be married at last."

"Fuck off," she says.

In my new passport photo I look stunned, as if someone has just hit me on the back of the head with a skillet, and I have yet to fall down. I've only been abroad once before, on the eighth-grade French class's summer trip to Paris.

The passport shows that I first entered the United Kingdom on March 2, 1990. By the time of the last stamp on the back page, dated October 28, 1999, I will have had three children. Whenever I take stock by asking myself that question—"What the hell happened to you?"—I remember that the answers to that question are, by and large, indexed in this passport. It is the table of contents to the most tumultuous ten-year period of my existence. It's as if someone told me to get a life at the end of the 1980s and I took them literally. Looking at the unshaven, stunned young man in the photo now, I can only think, You don't know the half of it, you git.

On the morning of March 2, I am sitting in a café in the Kings Road, waiting for my new girlfriend to come and get me. My friend Pat, who has since moved back to London, is once again my waiter.

She picks me up in her car. As she drives me back to her flat in Olympia, I watch London scroll past the passenger window while making the sort of unappreciative remarks one might expect from a first-time American visitor of no particular sophistication.

"All these 'TO LET' signs," I say. "Why hasn't anyone defaced them so they say 'TOILET'?"

"Because no one here is that stupid," she says.

"A lack of initiative, is what it is."

The ten days go by in a blur. I have no bearings; I'm always lost. She drags me round a series of indistinguishable pubs to show me to a series of friends. On one such occasion I am wearing an old St. Louis Cardinals T-shirt I found in a box of old clothes collected for a friend whose house had burned down—a shirt rejected by a homeless person with no possessions. "This is my new American boyfriend," she says, presenting me with two flat palms, "in his national costume."

I spend all my time trying not to look surprised by stuff, but every experience has something quietly remarkable about it. Cigarettes come out of the machine with your change taped to the outside of the box. There are more national newspapers than there are TV channels. Everybody has a tiny hotel fridge and no one ever suggests it's too early in the day to drink beer. London is unexpectedly old-fashioned and louche, and I am mostly charmed by it.

One night the English girl drives me to a Greek restaurant.

"We're meeting my friend Jason," she says as we pull up. "He's the last person I slept with before you."

"Are you kidding?" I said. "I can't go in there now."

"Don't be such a baby," she says. "Come on."

Something else unexpected happens during these ten days: we fight. Not the whole time, but more than twice. I cannot now remember anything about these arguments other than the impact they had on me. Our relationship was, in face-to-face terms, barely three weeks old. It seemed far too soon to have rubbed away the veneer of goodwill that comes with initial infatuation. Why are we arguing already? Either she is the most disagreeable person I've ever met, or I am the most infuriating person she's ever met (I should say that, after twenty years of marriage, it's still possible that both these things are true).

I am also profoundly annoyed because being happy and in love had been a major part of my holiday plans. I keep thinking: I took a week off work for this! I broke up with my girlfriend! I didn't come all this way just to visit the Tower of London.

Worst of all, she doesn't seem to share my fear that falling out at this early stage is reckless or a bad omen. She enters into these arguments without showing the slightest worry about the damage that might result. Maybe she doesn't care.

I've never before had romantic dealings with anyone quite so direct. When she gets angry she does not cry or attempt to explain her feelings of exasperation. Disagreeing with her is like facing an angry neighbor who has told you to turn down the music one too many times. Two months after we first met, she still scares the shit out of me.

Having committed myself to the high-wire act of a transatlantic relationship, I find myself struggling to cope with the hour-to-hour business of being together. I begin to suspect there is an element of sabotage in her attitude; maybe she sees the bickering as a kind way to euthanize a nonviable love affair. The day of my return flight is fast approaching, and we have no long-term plans. We have no plans at all.

When the final morning arrives, cold and soggy, it seems like the end. I make my own way to the airport in a state of bereaved resignation. I'm not at all sure the English girl is still my girlfriend. This, I realize, is what most long-distance relationships amount to: a brief, heedless romance, an expensive visit apiece, and a tacit acknowledgment of defeat. The English girl has a new job, and is about to buy a flat with a friend. She is embarking on a life in her own country that has no room for me in it. As the Gatwick Express crawls through South London, I think about what I'm going back to: my dead-end job, my stupid life, my tiny room, my gigantic, empty bed. The last place I want to be is home.

It's ironic, I think to myself as I glare through the window at a stately procession of back gardens, that a train service calling itself the Gatwick Express moves so slowly that I could keep up jogging along beside it. What a stupid country. After a few minutes the train comes to a complete halt. Twenty minutes later, it has still not moved.

I call her from the airport.

"I missed my flight," I say. There follows a brief, unbearable silence.

"Christ," she says, pausing to blow smoke. "Come back in on the train and I'll meet you at Victoria."

In comparison to the outward journey, the brisk thirty-minute ride to London is a mere flashback: suburban gardens and quilted scraps of wooded ground flash by, reversing, and to some extent undoing, the abortive first leg of my trip home. I'm prepared for her to give me a hard time for being an idiot, but as we drive back to the flat she's in a giddy mood.

"You picked a good day to miss a plane," she says. "*Reach for the Sky* is on telly."

So we spend the afternoon sitting on the floor with a bottle of Bulgarian wine, watching an old black-and-white film. The extra day feels like a reprieve, twenty-four hours of happiness robbed from an unpromising future. Having never seen *Reach for the Sky*, I'd been expecting a weepy romantic saga, not the life story of double-amputee fighter pilot Douglas Bader. It appears to be her favorite film of all time. I think this is probably when I know she is the one for me.

Midway through Douglas Bader's rehabilitation, her friend Miranda—the one she's supposed to be buying a flat with—rings to say she's pregnant. A little later she rings again to say she's getting married. In an instant, the future turns fluid.

I catch a flight home the next day; the day after that, I quit my job. I write a letter to my English girlfriend, telling her that as soon as I get my tin legs I'll be flying again.

That's my version, anyway. My wife remembers events slightly differently, insofar as she remembers them at all. When I reminded her of this particular turning point recently, she claimed not to recollect anything significant about it.

"You missed your flight," she said. "I remember that. Then you left the next day."

"And then I came back," I said. "In June."

"That's right," she says. "Were you made redundant or something?"

"No, I quit."

"Oh. With a view to what, exactly?"

2.

Are You Compatible?

Compatibility is a trait one tends to divine only in hindsight. Most relationships are themselves just a very slow way of discovering that you are incompatible. Or the other person may come to believe that you are incompatible, while you still think you're both perfectly compatible. That, of course, is the worst sort of incompatibility.

In my twenties I don't think I really believed in a level of compatibility that could withstand a punishment like marriage. If I liked someone and they liked me back, that was reason enough to embark on a romance for me. A relationship predicated on no other basis could easily last a year, or two, or until the girl in question decided she was more compatible with the guitarist of the band I was in.

I don't remember any of my prior relationships beginning with a sense that there was something predestined about its nature. They never kicked off under circumstances that could be described as auspicious—just opportune. Nor was there any particular sense of progress as one relationship followed another. That I went out with two

Cynthias in a row proves I had no grand design. I agreed to go out with the second one minutes after she made the same offer to my friend Mark and he turned her down. Later she said she actually fancied me more, but I never understood why, if that was the case, she asked him first. I suppose it's the kind of thing that happens to lots of fourteen-year-old boys. I was twenty-one. It took her a year to realize her mistake.

We are none of us in a position to select a partner based on the length of the relationship desired, the way you choose an airport car park based on the duration of your holiday. You can't predict a "long stay" or "mid stay" boyfriend ("short stay" is perhaps easier); the future will simply refuse to conform to your itinerary. And yet when a relationship does somehow manage to stand the test of time, casual observers will naturally assume that the seeds of its sustainability were sown at the start, that these two people were somehow destined to be together. What makes such a couple so perfectly compatible? Is it their many shared interests? Their similar backgrounds? A mutual sense of purpose? Are the two people in question polar but complementary opposites? Was the alignment sexual? Political? Delusional?

You cannot be married for twenty years without other people thinking there must be some trick to it. And for all I know, my marriage does have some secret knack for longevity. While I can't necessarily tell you what that secret is, I can tell you what it isn't.

We do not come from similar backgrounds. My wife is from London and the child of divorced parents. I am from suburban Connecticut and my parents stayed together. It is rare that a month goes by without my wife informing someone that I am not, on paper, her sort of thing at all.

When we met we didn't like the same music and there was barely a single book the both of us had read. We had no shared interests beyond smoking and drinking, and although we remained devoted to both for some years, we abandoned one of these key planks in our marital platform halfway through. It may not be long before we have to give up the other.

We are sexually compatible in the broadest sense, but from the very beginnings of our marriage there were the usual disagreements about the minimum number of "units" per calendar month that could be said to constitute connubial health. I'm sure my wife would say that we eventually reached an agreeable compromise on this delicate matter. She is, I suppose, entitled to her opinion.

Neither of us actually believes in anything as romantic as an instant connection, although I didn't even know this about my wife until recently, when I asked her for the purposes of this book if she believed in love at first sight.

"No," she said. "I don't even believe in love after several repeat viewings."

If we had any shared notion—indeed, any notion at all—about what the future held for the pair of us, it was a strong premonition that ours was a union doomed to failure, cursed by circumstance, geography, financial constraints, and the lack of any of the above compatibility signifiers.

In spite of all this, we did later learn that our mutual friends—there were two—had long been intrigued by the possibility of our meeting. The people who knew us both beforehand divined some potential spark between two strangers who lived on different continents, raising the possibility of a native affinity that was apparent, if not necessarily definable.

There are theories about the evolutionary advantages of monogamy—it helps with child-rearing, and the practice may stem from the threat of infanticide from competing adult males—but there isn't much hard evidence to suggest that biological imperatives lie behind a couple choosing one another, or help determine a relationship's success. In fact, the persistent belief that certain people are destined to be together may itself be a reason that relationships fail.

Long-term studies in the United States have suggested that married couples who subscribe to a "soul mates" model—a shared sense that their compatibility rests on some special romantic connection—are not only less likely to stay married than couples who take a more pragmatic view of the institution, but are also less happy. When an insistence that you "belong together" is the main plank of your relationship's contractual platform, it stands to reason that the reality of married life will prove disappointing. The feeling of belonging together is not self-sustaining. Nothing good about a marriage happens by itself.

The PAIR project, which examined 168 married couples over fourteen years, found that it was precisely this sort of disillusionment that led to people divorcing around the seven-year mark. The same study seemed to show that the most successful marriages are made between people whose personal contract emphasizes mutual respect, a frank appreciation of each other's weaknesses, and realistic expectations from the institution itself.

The psychologist Robert Epstein's ongoing study of arranged marriages suggests that a brokered match generally works out better than a relationship between two people who have chosen each other. In arranged marriages the amount of love a couple reports feeling for one another tends to increase over time. In most Western marriages, you will not be surprised to hear, the opposite happens.

Epstein isn't necessarily an advocate of

arranged marriage; he just believes virtually any two people can deliberately teach themselves to love one another, as long as they're both fully committed to the project. In practice my own marriage probably subscribes less to the "soul mates" model and more to a "cell mates" one, but I realize I'm not really selling the idea of wedded bliss with that admission.

And anyway, neither model quite dispenses with the notion of compatibility: an attraction strong enough to allow you to think about the daunting prospect of marriage in the first place, an affinity that makes your relationship a better bet than some others, an irrational emotional response that makes you break up with your girlfriend of four years a week after meeting an English girl in a red duffel coat. Could there actually be something deeper at work, something chemical? Something genetic, even?

In his book *The Compatibility Gene*, Daniel M. Davis reported on a curious study—the so-called sweaty T-shirt experiment. First performed by the Swiss zoologist Claus Wedekind in 1994, the experiment involved a group of students, forty-four males and forty-nine females. Wedekind first analyzed the students' DNA, in particular their major histocompatibility genes (MHCs). The group was then divided along gender lines. The men were told to wear plain cotton T-shirts for a certain period while abstaining from anything—

soap, sex, alcohol—that might alter their natural scent. After two days the shirts were placed in unmarked cardboard boxes with holes in them, and the forty-nine women were asked to rank the boxes by smell using three criteria: intensity, pleasantness, and sexiness.

Wedekind's initial results showed that the women preferred the T-shirts worn by men whose compatibility genes were most different from their own. Your MHCs contain the code to make your immune system, and the range you inherit—one set, or haplotype, from each parent—is, in a sense, your genetic identity. It's the "self" that your immune system checks against when distinguishing between your own cells and something "nonself" like a virus.

Although the results were controversial, the sweaty T-shirt experiment seemed to indicate that we unconsciously select mates whose MHCs would diversify the immune systems of any potential offspring, thereby increasing their chance of survival against disease.

No one quite understands the mechanism by which we might sniff out the individual genes of someone we meet at a party (especially through a fog of perfume, soap, and alcohol), but this hasn't stopped dating agencies from employing MHC typing as a matchmaking tool. One lab offering such testing to online dating services claims that "with genetically compatible people we feel that rare sensation of perfect chemistry."

I'm not sure there's a geneticist on the planet who would stand by that statement, but the advent of DNA testing for genetic compatibility raises the intriguing possibility that one might, for the sake of argument, find out if two people who had already been married for twenty years were actually meant for each other at the molecular level. Just because you can do it doesn't mean you should do it. But I did do it. It's okay—I'm a journalist. I did it for money.

To test your marital compatibility after two decades together seems, to say the least, a bit reckless. While I might well think that the length of the marriage itself constitutes proof of compatibility that no DNA sample can contradict, I am also worried about my wife reading the test results and saying, "Well *that* certainly explains a lot."

My wife's only fear has nothing to do with our possible incompatibility; she just doesn't want any needles stuck in her. Fortunately, to test your DNA all you have to do is put a little bit of your spit in the post.

"If I have to watch you do that," says my wife, "I'm going to be sick." I turn my back and continue drooling into the test tube. An attached lid flips over the funneled top, piercing a membrane and releasing a measured amount of blue pre-servative. After shaking up the samples and labeling them according to the instructions, I seal them in a pre-addressed envelope while quietly admiring how idiot-proof the whole process has been made. I'm halfway to the post box before I realize I've left out the signed consent forms.

It takes two weeks for the samples to be processed by a method I cannot begin to explain, during which time I worry ceaselessly. Without ever quite admitting it to myself, I have long suspected that romantic love—or at least the first flush of it—is some kind of biologically triggered delusion, one you might sum up with words as empty and meaningless as "that rare sensation of perfect chemistry."

As the date for the test results approaches I am seized by an irrational fear that the natural smell of my genes is actually quite off-putting, and that twenty years ago my wife fell in love with the brand of deodorant I used to use. Do they even still make it?

On further investigation I learn that the hormones in the contraceptive pill can interfere with a woman's response to olfactory signals. In the sweaty T-shirt experiment, women who were on the pill actually preferred the smell of men with compatibility genes similar to their own—they were getting it exactly wrong. I go in search of my wife, who I find sitting in the kitchen.

"Were you on the pill when you met me?" I

say. She looks up from the newspaper she's reading and stares at me.

"It's a bit late to ask me that now," she says. "But yes."

Oh my God, I think: Are the people at the lab going to tell her that she picked the wrong husband? While I don't actually believe you can find the perfect partner by sending your spit to a company in Switzerland—or that body odor is the start and finish of attraction—I do not underestimate the psychological force of being told there are rather better genetic matches out there for you than the git you married. Such news might not be easy to dismiss. Who knows? I'm finding it hard enough to imagine my reaction, much less my wife's. What have I done?

At the end of the fortnight we are both summoned to the Anthony Nolan lab in Hampstead to receive our results from Professor Steve Marsh. They don't analyze DNA for dating agencies at Anthony Nolan, but they use the same sort of testing to match tissue types for bone marrow transplantation. As we sit down in a conference room with Professor Marsh, I steel myself to receive bad news I won't understand.

Marsh explains a bit about the specific genes the testing looks for—genes that contain instructions to make proteins called human leukocyte antigens (HLAs). HLA proteins don't exist to facilitate online matchmaking, nor are they there to make bone marrow transplantation a pain in the arse. Their job is to fight infection.

"If you have a virus," says Marsh, "these are the molecules that are taking little bits of the virus and showing it to other cells and saying, 'Is this me? Or is it foreign?' If it's foreign, the cell is killed."

Some HLA molecules are better at snatching up certain protein fragments than others; people with a particular HLA type have increased resistance to the HIV virus. Some HLA genes, however, make you more susceptible to certain disorders. None of this sounds terribly sexy, but it makes sense that a decent spread of HLA types would be of benefit, and that a member of the opposite sex who's got some HLAs you don't have would make a good partner, and therefore might possibly smell more attractive to you.

Marsh has good news. My wife and I share just one HLA type (an allele, as it is called): HLA-A*32:01:01. The rest are different, a level of diversity which makes us a good genetic match, and allegedly highly desirable to one another. "If the whole sniffing-your-mate-out thing is to be believed," says Marsh, "then you've managed to sniff out a good mate." It's not clear which one of us he is talking to.

My overall HLA makeup turns out to be fairly common, which means, I suppose, that a broad range of women of European Caucasian extraction would, upon meeting me, find me inexplicably unattractive (a lifetime of anecdotal evidence does, to some extent, support this theory). Conversely, it also means there are two perfect tissue matches for me on the bone marrow donor register in the UK, and five more in the US. Being common has its advantages.

Fortunately for our progeny, my wife comes from less common stock. So uncommon, in fact, that her HLA-B*27 allele doesn't end in a bunch of numbers, but with two XXs. A footnote at the bottom of her report says, "The HLA-B locus appears to be novel, with the novel allele likely to be a new B*27. Further work is currently being undertaken to confirm this finding." Professor March confirms that this means what I think it means: my wife has a B*27 allele that no one has ever seen before, one that does not exist on a worldwide database of twenty-two million recorded tissue types. She is, as I always suspected, more than rare: she is weird, unique, a one-off. And I smelled her first.

3.

Getting Married: Why Would You?

In my first summer in Britain I get taken to a lot of weddings. I feel out of place for a number of reasons. Back in America I had never attended the wedding of a friend. Nobody I knew had ever got married. Here in the UK, people my age hardly seem to be doing anything else. I'm happy for them, but I do not feel like someone heading in that direction at all. I'm at the very start of a relationship, and its long-term prospects are a little shaky. I'm not embarking on a new life so much as running away from my old one. Responsibility, commitment, adulthood: I've deliberately put as much distance—an ocean—between me and all that stuff as possible. I'm here to have fun. I'll go home when it all goes wrong, and suffer the consequences then.

The main reason I feel out of place is that I don't know anyone. I am foreign. In the past I may have sabotaged relationships through my maddening aloofness, but now—out of bald self-interest—I am as clingy a boyfriend as you could want. Wherever my girlfriend goes, I go; wherever she stands, I stand slightly behind her.

But at wedding receptions we usually get put at different tables. I sit in front of place cards with the words "plus one" on them, in the company of strangers. I sit with flower girls, vicars, the groom's nanny, ex-neighbors of the bride's parents. People don't believe me when I tell them that I was once seated next to a pug, and that I didn't really mind because there was no need for small talk and he had such beautiful manners. Perhaps I am exaggerating a little. He had beautiful manners for a dog.

I have nothing against all these people who are getting married, at my age. It just seems so heedless, this headlong leap into the future. What makes them think they're ready for it? Why the hurry? What's the point?

In the meantime I am starting to wonder if my new girlfriend and I are actually compatible. Our relationship began as a sort of verbal sparring match—with me losing most of the time. Initially I was fine with this; it was amusing. In some ways it was the sort of relationship I'd always dreamed of—a spiky, muscular exchange that kept both parties on their toes. The first time I saw *Who's Afraid of Virginia Woolf?* I was actually envious of the dynamic (I've seen it since, quite recently, and I now get that it's not supposed to be tremendous fun).

But as we spend more time in the confines of her flat, perpetually low on funds, the sparring often gets combative. She can become disagreeable and hard to reach without much warning. As much as I admire her refusal to suffer fools gladly, I prefer it when the fool is someone other than me.

She can also suddenly turn fragile if the wrong button is accidentally pushed. I find it difficult to respect someone's forthrightness and their feelings at the same time, and I am aware that my increasing tendency to be at once defensive, cautious, and needy is not an attractive thing in a man.

My lack of independence doesn't help matters. I'd run out of money not long after I'd arrived. My mental map of London is confined to a circle with a half-mile radius; I never go far on my own. The relationship is the same: everything outside its claustrophobic center, where two people are arguing about the correct pronunciation of "beret," is uncharted territory. She's supposed to be my girlfriend, but I sometimes feel as if I'm just trying to navigate my way round a woman I don't understand at all.

At the time it didn't occur to me that I was learning, through a tortuous process of trial and error, to be a grown-up. I just thought English women were really weird.

I have a photograph from that first summer that sits on the shelf behind my desk. It's just a creased snap, unframed, one I rescued from a drawer full of pictures that never made it onto any walls or into any albums. It shows both of us lying side by side in the long matted grass near a Cornish cliff, on top of the same red duffel coat she wore the night we met. My arms are wrapped round her from behind. She is smiling, her half-lidded eyes gazing sleepily at the camera lens. I look as if I might be asleep.

I like this photograph because it is a lie. I remember clearly that she woke up that morning in a tricky mood, and that we argued on and off for most of the day. We argued right before that picture was taken, and right after. It actually captures a moment of supreme neediness on my part, and her smile is nothing but a brief, wry acknowledgment of her reluctance to tolerate my display of affection even for the time it takes a shutter to open and close.

You can't tell that from the picture, though. It just looks like two happy people lying on some grass. That's probably why I never put it in a frame, but it's also why I keep it where I can see it.

Less than half the population is married. A total of 231,490 people got married in England and Wales in 2009, which sounds a lot but was the lowest annual figure since 1895, and not much more than half the 1972 number. Cohabiting, meanwhile, has doubled since 1996. That makes me feel old, because I was already married in 1996.

There are many good reasons not to get married. It costs, on average, £16,000 in the UK ($28,000). Divorce, a disease for which marriage is a necessary precondition, is also expensive, and your chances of avoiding it aren't great. Roughly 40 percent of UK marriages fail.

If you are already living happily together as a couple, the change in status can hardly be said to be worth the outlay. There are some recently introduced tax advantages for the lawfully wedded, but you'd still have to be married for 106 years to break even. In terms of its impact on your personal life, marriage is much the same as cohabitation. I've tried both, and there isn't a tremendous amount of difference. Either way, on the subject of what should happen to a towel when you're done using it, you will always enjoy the benefit of a second opinion.

In any case, there is nothing wrong with your cohabitational arrangement that marriage is going to fix. The PAIR project's findings showed that among the couples who divorced soonest, a high percentage got married because they thought a wedding would somehow improve an already troubled relationship.

Marriage will, as numerous studies have indicated, improve both your health and your longevity, especially if you're a man (contrary to popular belief, marriage doesn't actually reduce the life expectancy of women; it extends it, just not as much as it does for men). Never-married men are three times more likely to die of cardiovascular disease than married men. Married men also have better cancer survival rates. But divorced men die sooner than married men, and you can't be divorced unless you get married first.

Most people have particular and deeply personal reasons for wanting to get married, and my primary motivation was, I like to think, as good as any: the Home Office forced my hand. Couples who live together without getting married will sometimes say things like, "We don't need a piece of paper from the government to validate our relationship." Well, I did.

From the beginning, being together proves difficult. Every time my six-month tourist visa nears its expiration, I have to go back to the States and make arrangements to return. It's both expensive and heart-wrenching. Over the two years that my relationship with my English girlfriend develops, my relationship with the people at immigration deteriorates markedly. Each time I hand over my passport they seem less charmed by my tale of true love. My reasons for entering the UK strike them as implausible. They think I'm working in Britain illegally, and say as much.

In fact, all the traveling back and forth makes it impossible to secure proper employment in either country. I am broke. The periods in America are the hardest to endure, months spent living with my parents. They are supportive, but also quite clearly of the opinion that I am fucking up my life, squandering it in six-month chunks. Whenever I'm home I take odd jobs—anything, including painting my dad's office—until I earn enough money for a cheap airline ticket. In an effort to impress the immigration officers with my continued commitment to US residency, I always show up with a return ticket on a flight a fortnight hence. It's usually nonrefundable, so I chuck it.

Every time I come back, they grill me for longer, make plainer their suspicions, and threaten to send me straight home. I am a bag of nerves for weeks before each visit. Some people are afraid to fly; I am afraid to land.

On my arrival on March 24, 1992, I am held at immigration for over an hour, left on a bench next to a guy who has no passport at all and refuses to tell anyone what country he's come from. It does not feel like a lucky bench. The immigration officer who finally deals with me is professionally unpleasant, like a disappointed geometry teacher. He treats me to a long and disheartening lecture about my unsuitability for admission, before suddenly relenting and letting me through; it's eerily reminiscent of the day I got my driver's license. The stamp in my passport is extra large and contains specific restrictions and the official's handwritten ID number. I'm pretty certain I have exhausted the forbearance of the United Kingdom.

This episode overshadows our reunion. I am delighted to have slipped through, but aware it may well be the last time I'll get away with it. It seems quite possible that after two years our relationship has finally run out of road.

There hardly seems enough time for my girlfriend and me to decide what should happen next. To start with, we do nothing. April and May drift by. Finally, in mid-June, we sit down together, me at the little drop-leaf table in the kitchen, her on the worktop, to discuss the future.

So daunting is the prospect of a wedding, much less a marriage, that the first option my girl-friend puts on the table is that we split up and live out the remainder of our lives on separate continents. As unpalatable as this idea is, I have to admit it sounds marginally less horrible than the prospect of having engagement photos taken. After an hour of circular debate, we arrive at what seems a dead end.

"So that's it," she says. "We're getting married."

"I suppose," I say.

"Never mind," she says, crossing the kitchen to

light a fag on the stove. "We can always get divorced."

Given our deep mutual reluctance to take the plunge, it would be insane for me to make any grand claims favoring marriage over simply living together for a very long time. They are very different arrangements legally—at present cohabitation comes with no rights or advantages at all—and of course they are slightly different constructs emotionally. With one a shared sense of commitment agglomerates over a long period of time, as two lives become increasingly intertwined; with the other you get all the commitment squared away on a specific day, generally before you've had lunch. But for the sake of argument I'll presume that in the long term the result is much the same. If you resisted the pressure to have a wedding, good for you. You probably saved a lot of money. I, on the other hand, have four salad bowls.

I will say only this about the trauma of actually getting married: it may be something you never thought you'd be interested in, and something you imagine to be painfully embarrassing while you are doing it (you imagine right), but afterward you will consider it a life-changing ordeal from which you emerged stronger, an ordeal that, for all its hideousness, created a special, unshakable bond between you and your partner. In this sense getting married is, I imagine, a lot like agreeing to do *Dancing on Ice*: you'll end up being pleased with yourself for enduring something terrifying, difficult, and unutterably naff.

When she finishes telling her mother the news on the phone, we go to see her father. I ask him for his daughter's hand while he is showing me the progress of the work on his new loft extension. We are alone, standing on joists, looking down into the room below us. I consider the likelihood of him pushing me through.

"How are you going to keep my daughter in the style to which she has become accustomed?" he asks, looking stern. I don't know that he's been tipped off by my future mother-in-law, that he already has champagne on ice downstairs, that he's only messing with me. I briefly contemplate jumping.

When I speak to my mother, I try to play down the whole business as a tiresome piece of administration, an elaborate exchange of paperwork which must be done at short notice. I don't want to put anyone to any trouble just because I am obliged to jump through some bureaucratic hoops. Because my mother is a devout Catholic, I am hoping she won't think a register office wedding counts, and therefore won't feel she's missing much. I suggest that after enduring whatever dry little ceremony constitutes the bare legal requirement for marriage in Britain, we will travel to the States, where she can arrange a blessing and throw an embarrassing party for us. There is a silence at the other end.

"You can do whatever you want," she says. "But whatever it is, we're coming over for it."

Within weeks of us setting a date—just three months hence—my mother has invited sufficient relatives to fill a minibus. In addition to our booking at Chelsea register office, my future mother-in-law has secured, on my mother's behalf, an hour slot in a Catholic church in Wimbledon, and a friendly priest who has agreed to put us through the pre-Cana period of instruction that will allow us to be married in the eyes of God. To my surprise, my new fiancée agrees to all of this without protest. Perhaps she believes that if the marriage is going to stick it must be done to the satisfaction of all concerned. I don't know; I'm not asking a lot of questions at this point. I think the fact that in many ways it's no longer about what we want makes us both feel a little better.

As we pull up outside the rectory for our first meeting with the priest, I realize I am far more anxious than she is. My stance regarding God is akin to the author Peter Ackroyd's position on ghosts. "I don't believe in ghosts," he once wrote, "but I am frightened of them." I am scared of the God I don't believe in, and also of priests. I'm worried my double agnosticism—doubt, doubtfully held—will be transparent enough to get us disqualified. She has no such fear, and this also scares me. I look over at her as she turns off the headlights.

"You're not going to suddenly say that Jesus is a pillock, or anything like that, are you?" I say.

"I don't think so," she says.

"And don't say, 'If it doesn't work out, we can always get divorced.' "

"We can, though."

"I know. But he might not find your robust outlook as charming as I do."

"Christ."

"Don't say 'Christ,' " I say. "Not in there."

In fact Father Jim is welcoming, kind, and prone to reward a half hour's earnest chat with an extremely strong gin and tonic. Our meetings with him are the only time we ever discuss topics including love, commitment, children, and, more generally, the future, with anyone. My wife-to-be, who has virtually no experience of religion and is therefore free to take from it what she wishes, finds it all rather bracing. For me, Catholicism remains an unfinished school assignment, a dropped subject. I sweat a lot during these meetings, but I am grateful that someone took the time to impress upon us the seriousness of the whole undertaking.

He is not the only person we have meetings with, though. We have meetings about flowers, about venues, about food, booze, music, and printed invitations. I'd somehow imagined that our whirlwind engagement might relieve us of some of the stresses associated with a big wedding, but it just means we have to do the same stuff faster. We do have engagement photos taken—I look like a frightened potato in them—and our pending nuptials are announced in a national newspaper. It's going to look terribly convincing, this sham marriage we've hastily arranged just so we can stay together forever.

I am prone to nightmares in which I find myself back at school or still in college, suddenly facing the prospect of sitting a final exam for a class I signed up for but never attended, taught by a teacher who would not recognize me (they may be dreams, but they're based on true stories). At the point where the full consequences of my unpreparedness are about to be made plain I wake up and discover, to my immense relief, that I am middle-aged, and therefore closer to the sweet release of death than I am to tenth-grade chemistry.

Waking on my wedding day, the reverse happens: I had been dreaming of mundane things, only to open my eyes and find myself in a foreign country where I'm about to get married. My life's greatest test to date is scheduled for eleven thirty a.m., and I could not be less ready.

I have borrowed a dark blue suit from my friend Bill, without trying it on first. He's much taller than me; the trousers, it transpires, are three or four inches too long. Only the night before, my friend Jennifer had had to come round and staple new hems into place. I need to step into the trousers very gingerly in the morning to avoid undoing her work.

My memory of the next four or five hours is dangerously unreliable, and full of blank spots. It's a good thing there are pictures. My imminent wife and I spent the night apart—she at her mother's, me in the flat. I don't remember meeting up the next morning outside the Chelsea register office at all; only the part where I watched her write out a check to cover the cost of the ceremony in a back office. I remember stepping from the office into a venue area—a big sitting room, really—crammed with about forty people I either knew or was related to, and trying not to catch anyone's eye. I recall a bit of the rigorously bland language in the vow I recited: "I do solemnly declare that I know not of any lawful impediment why I, Robert Timothy Dowling, may not be joined in matrimony to . . ." I was basically petitioning to get married because I could not think of a solid legal reason to stop myself.

A lunch follows the ceremony, followed by a big party in a pub and a night in a posh hotel. The first real test of our marriage doesn't come until the next morning, when we have to get married again. After getting to bed at about four a.m., I am up and waiting for a taxi at seven thirty. My Catholic wedding is at ten, and by prior arrangement I am attending the preceding mass with my family. My wife is to arrive later for the ceremony. I am badly hungover, nervous and shaking. I am in no fit state to get married and, had I not already been married, I might have got cold feet. But I didn't. Reader, I married her, again. I married the shit out of her.

The next day, we fly to Naples. It seems odd to leave behind such a large collection of normally far-flung friends, relatives, and in-laws—an assemblage that will never recur—while they're all having fun in London, but we need to go on honeymoon. It's booked, and more important, I can only apply for indefinite leave to remain from outside the UK. We are leaving the country so I can get back in.

Our priority in Naples is a visit to the British vice-consul, the only man in the area with the authority to approve my reentry into the UK, excepting, I suppose, the consul. We turn up with our marriage certificate, some required paperwork, and a selection of specially taken Polaroid wedding photos, and we are prepared to hold hands if it will help. The vice-consul waves away our photos, signs our papers, and gives us tea. He regards our case as a welcome distraction, he says, from his regular duties, which seem to revolve largely around repatriating penniless students.

The business is completed in under an hour. The remaining nine days of our honeymoon on the Amalfi Coast stretch uncertainly before us.

In the days when couples had tightly restricted access to each other before the wedding, a honeymoon made sense. If you've already spent two years living in a tiny flat together, the honeymoon does not coincide with the honeymoon period. Nine days seems like an awful lot of enforced togetherness, especially when you've just embarked upon a project that quietly terrifies you both.

As a young married couple in a foreign country, you feel not just alone but positively quarantined, strolling through the unfamiliar streets of Positano together like two people who share a rare disease. It might well prove an instructive and reinvigorating break from the day-to-day drift of an established relationship, but ten days into a marriage is not a good time to discover you've run out of conversation. Under the circumstances, we do the only sensible thing: we run out of money instead.

In hindsight we could have blamed a lack of preparation, but what really happened amounted to a failure of leadership. Whenever we'd been together in America I'd invariably made the arrangements. In London my wife had organized everything while I watched, agog, as if my life were happening in a museum.

On neutral territory, however, neither of us takes charge. Nobody keeps proper count of the cash, tots up the receipts, or attempts to square our spending with the number of days left. The exchange rate is often discussed, but never quite mastered. Perhaps we both feel that the hard-nosed financial pragmatism a marriage requires shouldn't start until after the honeymoon ends. As a team we prove to be both indecisive and extravagant, switching hotels on a whim, hiring boats without checking the price, and ordering expensive drinks on the beach. We had been gifted a tidy pile of cash as a reward for getting married, but it runs through our fingers without us even feeling it. This is before—right before—it was possible to put your bank card into a cash machine anywhere in the world and receive handfuls of the local money. In 1992 that sort of preposterous convenience is still a far-off dream. Even a bank wire transfer takes three days.

Somehow, with two days to go, we wake up in a hotel on Capri with the equivalent of £30 in lira between us. It is not enough to pay the bill we've run up already. In fact it is only enough for one of us to take the boat back to Naples to beg some money from the only person we know there.

"You have to go," I say to my wife, bravely. "He's *your* vice-consul."

"I'll be back," she says. "Don't eat anything."

So I sit in a room I cannot check out of because

I cannot settle the bill, wondering if I'll ever see my wife again. It occurs to me that Naples is not the sort of city to which one sends a woman alone on an errand. If anything happens to my wife I will have to live with the guilt. I have an urge to go after her, but then I remember I don't have the money to cross the bay. I am paralyzed by worry, although my mind somehow finds the where-withal to ask itself whether a dip in the pool might help.

Finally, at sunset, my wife returns.

"He was very nice about it," she says. "He gave me some money from the distressed seamen's fund."

We pay our bill and return to the mainland in search of a room close to the bus station, so we can get to the airport first thing and put this whole honeymoon business behind us. The hotel we select is so cheap that it doesn't even start until the second floor of the run-down building it occupies, and you need to put money in the lift to make it go up. It's just the sort of place two distressed seamen might spend their last night in Naples.

The front desk is a man in a hat sitting at a folding table on the landing. He also sells beer, fags, and soap. But the room has huge windows and a fresco covering the whole ceiling, apart from a bit in the corner where they cut into the plaster to install a shower cubicle. We sit in the window and take a picture of ourselves with a timer, looking out onto the street at dusk. When I want to remember that I had a romantic honeymoon in Naples with the woman I love, that's the one I look at.

In a lot of ways it does not feel as if we're genuinely married until we turn up at passport control with our paperwork. There are a few more questions, a bit of a wait, some instructions I am too nervous to take in, and finally, a stamp in my passport that grants me a full year to sort out my new status. At last, I'm an immigrant.

"Now you just have to see the doctor," says the official.

"The what?" I say.

I am led to a little examination room in a weird backstage area, where I remove my shirt for Dr. Gatwick, a weary-looking man with a mildly sinister bearing.

"Any diseases worth mentioning?" he asks. If I had any, I think, I wouldn't mention them to you.

"No," I say.

He listens to my chest, takes my blood pressure, and asks me a few more questions. Then I am allowed to put my shirt back on and rejoin my wife on British soil. Dr. Gatwick's seal of approval is the final hurdle to married life, or at least that's how it seems until we are safely on the train to London, and I realize that virtually all the hurdles are still ahead of us.

4.

How to Be Wrong

Take a moment to cast your eyes around my domain: this blasted promontory, wracked by foul winds, devoid of life, of cheer, of comfort. This is my special place—my fortress of solitude. I've been coming here on and off for the last twenty years. Welcome, my friend, to the moral high ground.

Sit down. Do you want some tea? I'm afraid they only do oat milk up here. It's the moral high ground—what did you expect? There are some salt-free rice cakes on the shelf there. They're a bit joyless, but help yourself—just make sure you put tenpence in the honesty box.

What were we talking about? Oh yeah: so, earlier today my wife was giving me a hard time about not putting the ladder back in the shed. I told her it was pointless keeping the ladder in the shed because I use it all the time, almost exclusively in the house, and that it was much more convenient and sensible to store it at the back of the cupboard under the stairs, like we used to before we got the shed. And by the way: Why wasn't I consulted about the switch in the first place?

My wife responded by saying that, at any rate, the ladder didn't live in the middle of the sitting room, where it had been all weekend, and went on to imply that I was just being lazy and also, quite possibly, a twat. Then I said: Okay, this is not about the ladder anymore. This is about the proper way to conduct discourse between adults. I refuse on principle—on principle!—to engage with a person who would resort to such a personal attack. Someone has to make a stand against this sort of thing, I said, and for that reason no ladders will be moved today. And that's how I ended up here, on the moral high ground. It's like a VIP room for idiots.

I don't remember the subject of the first big argument I had with my wife, only its aftermath. I'm sure it began, as in the example above, with some trivial domestic dispute—a failure to do something on my part, let's assume—which quickly escalated into a frank exploration of my inadequacies.

It is perhaps a year before we are married. At some point during the argument I decide my character is being assailed in a manner incompatible with my dignity. I say as much, and storm out of her flat, slamming the door as hard as I can behind me, heading straight for the moral high ground. I stomp downstairs and slam the front door, not quite as hard, because its maintenance is covered by a costly leasehold agreement.

I stand on the front step for a moment, breathing hard and basking in the hot glow of my righteous anger, until it dawns on me that I have no money and don't know anyone in London who would automatically take my side in this or any other matter. I toy with the idea of going back upstairs to pick up the fight where I left off—as if I'd just thought of another point worth making—but I don't have any keys. The hot glow wears off. It's cold and windy, and my dramatic exit did not afford an opportunity to grab a coat on the way out. I look up and down the darkening street. Wherever the moral high ground is, I think, it ain't out here. I quickly realize that the only decision left to make is whether I count to thirty or sixty before swallowing my pride. I settle on sixty, give up at forty-five, congratulate myself on my willingness to compromise, and push the bell.

"Hello?" she says.

"Can I come back in?" I say.

"Sorry, who is this?"

Since that day I've gradually learned to be more cautious about sticking my flag on any summit of self-righteousness. Claiming the moral high ground is, in the end, just a tactic, one that trial and error has demonstrated doesn't work very well on my wife. If, for example, I were to leap out of a vehicle my wife was driving during a heated argument—ostensibly because I, a man of quiet sense, could no longer share such a confined space with someone so unreasonable—I know she would not creep along the pavement with the passenger window down, begging me to get back in while conceding that she may have spoken rashly. I've tested this, and experience has taught me that she will actually speed off before I've had a chance to shut the door. She will not come back, even if it's raining, nor will she subsequently ring me to find out how I'm coping with my choices.

A relationship expert I once interviewed over the phone about argument techniques (I was looking for shortcuts and cheats, to be honest) asked me, "Do you want to be right, or do you want to have sex tonight?" At the time the whole idea of ceding one's claim to the moral high ground in order not to jeopardize the prospect of future intercourse struck me as highly unethical, although I had to admit it also sounded like the sort of thing I would do. Still, it wasn't fair. Why can't I have sex *and* be right? In a perfect world, my wife would want to sleep with me *because* I'm right.

The relationship expert, much as it pains me to say it, had a point. In the context of marriage, a moral victory is something you'll invariably end up celebrating on your own. If you're going to get on in married life—if you're going to have sex ever—you've got to learn to lose an argument. And to do that, you've got to learn how to be wrong. I honestly don't know where the work of being a good husband finishes, but I have an idea where it starts. It starts with counting to sixty, giving up at forty-five, and pushing the bell.

Unfortunately being wrong does not come easy to men, even when they are very, very wrong. A man will go to great lengths just to avoid being put in a position where he might be obliged to express uncertainty.

"Why don't you just say 'I don't know'?" my wife will sometimes shout after I've just spent ten minutes trying to create the opposite impression. What does she expect? If you don't want my impersonation of expertise, don't ask me questions I can't answer.

In the company of other men, being wrong is almost impossible to live down; that's why we spend so much time debating points that can't be settled one way or another—the hypothetical and the unknowable: the outcome of future sporting events, alternative tactics that might have affected the outcome of past sporting events, the true motivations of politicians, economic forecasts, etc. That's why fishing is such a perfect communal activity for men: you can spend an entire day speculating about what might be happening underwater. Once upon a time we could also argue over areas of shared historical and scientific ignorance, but the smartphone put paid to all that:

Circumference of the sun? 4,366,813 kilometers. Plantagenet kings? Got it right here, mate.

Women tend be more forgiving about wrongness. Some women, in my experience, will even defer to a man's pronouncements on a subject when he's clearly wrong—when everyone else in the room is thinking: You're wrong—if only to avoid denting his fragile ego in public.

My wife is not one of those women. She does not draw a big distinction between denting my fragile ego in public and denting it at home. It's one of the reasons I love her, and it's also one of the reasons I won't play tennis with her. It can't be a bad thing for a man to learn to admit his mistakes with grace, or even, initially, without grace.

While arguing is inevitable in a marriage, protracted disputes can be damaging to a relationship, and are often avoidable. There usually comes a time in the middle of a heated argument when you realize you would rather be doing something else: watching TV perhaps, or eating. But if you have any sense at all you will not attempt to suspend hostilities by saying, "Ooh, that thing is about to start on BBC2," or "You know what? I could really go for some M&M's right now."

Conversely it is rare to be struck, midargument, by the sudden realization that you are wrong.

That tends to happen much later, when you're sitting by yourself trying to figure out why you didn't win. It's too late to be wrong then.

Over many years I have learned the trick of amalgamating these two different types of epiphany. When you begin to lose interest in an argument either because you're hungry or bored or you've simply run out of steam, scan your brain for ways in which you could be wrong. This can be difficult for men—at first it may even feel as if your brain won't allow it—but this handy checklist should give you some clue as to the error of your ways:

SEVEN WAYS IN WHICH YOU MIGHT BE WRONG

1. *The Wrongness of Omission.* Have you deliberately withheld some evidence that supports the counter position? Introduce it as if you think it will help you, and then sit back and allow yourself to be taken apart.

2. *The Wrongness of Not Listening.* This has the advantage of almost always being true—you probably haven't been listening properly. You need to apologize, and then start listening, but that's all you have to do. Your contribution to the debate has finished. From now on, just nod.

3. *The Wrongness of Forgetting Your Original Purpose.* Arguments often lead you down little

strategic alleyways in search of short-term advantage, and it's easy to lose your way, especially if feelings are running high. But it's perfectly feasible to close your rant with the words, "and I've now forgotten why I even started this sentence!" If you allow your partner to reassemble the broken pieces of your argument for you, you will almost always end up with a more charitable interpretation of your logic than you deserve.

4. *The Wrongness of Underestimating Your Partner's Emotional Investment in the Issue.* This is the point at which you say, "I had no idea you felt so strongly about this," although what you probably mean is, "I've just realized I don't feel strongly about this at all." It's not your fault. Righteous anger is an opportunistic emotion—it can desert you at weird times.

5. *The Wrongness of Making It All About You.* It is rare for my wife and me to have a serious argument in which she does not at some stage say, "It has to be all about you, doesn't it?" In my extensive experience it's almost impossible to respond to such a challenge without making your answer All About You.

6. *The Wrongness of Offering an Ultimatum.* Whoops! Did you just draw a line in the sand? I think we both know you didn't mean to do that. When has brinkmanship ever worked for you in the past? My wife never blinks in these matters:

she knows I'm going all in with the argumentative equivalent of a pair of fours.

7. *The Wrongness of Being a Bit of a Cock.* All you have to say in this case is, "Perhaps I'm being a bit of a cock about this, but . . ." You might get a denial in return, although you shouldn't hold your breath.

Now all you have to do is find a way to acknowledge your error and give up. This is not a simple matter of saying, "Hang on a minute—I think I'm wrong!" and flicking on the TV. If you're going to be wrong, you've got to look wrong, even if that means mimicking a last-ditch attempt to save face.

Use whatever technique works best for you. Say "huh" dismissively and then let an awkward silence bloom. Or fold your arms, sit down, and stare at your shoes for a full minute—a classic. Try conceding in a way that doesn't sound at all conciliatory, by saying something such as "I'm wrestling with the unattractive possibility that you may have a point."

Here's one I use a lot, even now: I just say, "Whatever."

"Whatever" has a reputation as a meaningless piece of conversational shorthand, but it's actually terribly useful when conceding an argument. It acknowledges someone's right to an opinion without necessarily giving it credence, and, depending on your inflection, it can also imply that while life is too important to waste time fighting, your willingness to make peace— to be the bigger person—comes at some emotional cost. Best of all, it does all this gracelessly. The other person will assume that having lost your case on points, you are seeking to abandon the discussion before a humiliating climbdown becomes necessary. With "whatever," everybody walks away with something.

One of the great tactical advantages of admitting you're wrong is that in marriage nobody wants to be a bad winner. If you love someone it's impossible to draw much pleasure from forcing them to admit a mistake. The very few times I've actually won an argument I've noticed a strange hollow feeling in the pit of my stomach which somehow robs the moment of all satisfaction. And that is not how I want to feel at the end of an argument. That's how I want my wife to feel.

5.

Am I Relevant?

Men, you may have heard, are fast becoming outmoded. Permanent shifts in the economy and our social structures have created new employment opportunities and lifestyle options for women, rendering the human male obsolete. The market doesn't need us and, more signifi-cantly, women don't need us either. As far as women are concerned, men are useless. And a husband, from a woman's point of view, is just a useless man on a long lease. Who will want to marry you, now the End of Men is nigh? What can men do, at this stage of the game, to make themselves indispensable to society, and to womankind?

The problem, it seems, is that men's tradi-tional cultural capital—breadwinning, repressing emotions, etc.—no longer has much trade-in value. Women have colonized the workplace without ceding any domestic territory. Men have been slow to adapt to the new dispensation. Our most valuable resource—sperm—is both less potent than it used to be and more widely available than ever. I think you can get sperm from Amazon. Now that the bottom has dropped out of the sperm market, men must diversify while they still have options. Nobody wants to get caught with a load of worthless sperm on his hands. You know what I mean.

This is hardly unfamiliar territory. You won't get very far in life as a man without someone at work trying to make you feel irrelevant. Remaining indispensable at work is, of course, a simple matter of ensuring that your holiday replacement is a fool. This tactic is not generally recommended in marriage—you're not really supposed to take time off—but the same cunning should be applied to your overall gender relevance strategy.

The biggest obstacle to relevance, as the chart below illustrates, is that the old standards by which a husband's worth was measured no longer apply:

Being a Good Husband: 1950	Being a Relevant Husband: 2014
Every time you go out for cigarettes, you come back.	Every time you're sent out for espresso pods and tampons, you come back with the right sort.
You are the primary breadwinner.	You are the primary bread-baker.

78

Your main role is to provide.	Your main role is to provide answers at the school quiz, thanks to your extensive knowledge of US state capitals and Marvel Comics heroes.
You never cry.	You cry only when you think it will work.
You put on a tie to change a tire.	You put on a bicycle helmet to go to the shops.
You're good enough at plumbing to save hiring a professional.	You're good enough at polynomials to save hiring a maths tutor.
You know to keep married life and your various extramarital flings separate.	You know to keep whites and colors separate.

Regaining a sense of purpose is a vital first step to relevance. Modern masculinity is not a role per se; it's more of a patchwork of disparate talents, specialist knowledge, nonlateral thinking, and a handy lack of people skills. You must become a troubleshooter, ready to solve problems and fill gaps. Do not be afraid to step in wherever you think you can be of use. Don't wait—get out there and make yourself count. I don't know what your particular niche skills are, but here are some of mine:

Whistling loudly. Even today, with the End of Men almost upon us, I still don't meet many women who can whistle really loudly. I often see them in the park in the morning, making a pathetic flutey noise that their dogs can easily pretend not to hear. I guess if you don't learn to whistle properly by a certain age, you're never going to pick it up. This skill gap opens a vital window of opportunity for men. I don't like to brag, but when I stick two fingers in my mouth and blow, all the dogs look my way. I haven't quite figured out how to monetize this skill yet, but I'm hoping to use it to sell ads or something. I need to act quickly, though. Apparently you can just buy whistles in shops.

Monotasking. There are plenty of women out there who can hold down high-pressure jobs while simultaneously looking after children, baking cakes, and training for triathlons, but you know what they don't have? Focus. If there's anything men are good at, it's doing one thing to the exclusion of all other things, until the task in question is either completed or mostly completed. I don't wash up. I wash up the baking tray until that baking tray is so clean you could sell it on eBay under the description "like new." Afterward, if there's any hot water left, I might do the colander as well. If you want someone who can make work calls, write computer code, and deworm a cat at the same time, get a woman. If, however, you need someone to gouge all the old wax out of the base of a candlestick, then only a man will do.

Agreeing about curtains. Sometimes when you're choosing curtains you want advice from someone who says things like, "Love the color, not sure about the pinch pleats" or "The pattern goes well with the sofa, but are they maybe a bit heavy for summer?" Other times, however, you just want someone who'll say, "Yeah, fine, whatever." If it's the latter you require, please don't hesitate to call me.

Making fire. Arguably the smartest thing man ever did was learn to make fire. Definitely the second smartest thing we did was to keep the technique a secret from women. Coaxing flame from wood and charcoal is still considered men's work, even if nothing else is. Be poised to light the barbecue when asked, and do it when no one is looking. This would be a very bad moment in history for women to find out how easy it is.

Freelance fact delivery. I know some things. Would you like to know them too? Random information disgorged, all day, every day. No need to ask, just drift within earshot.

Professional Goldilocks. While women continue to rise to prominence across most employment sectors, they remain hampered by a gender-wide insensitivity to extremes of hot and cold. If you've ever seen a women handle a mug straight from the dishwasher at the end of its cycle, you'll know what I mean. With their weird tolerance of overhot baths and underheated houses, women simply cannot be relied upon to gauge appropriate temperatures. Fairy tales are lovely, but if you really want to know when your porridge is "just right," don't hire a little curly-haired girl. Get a man in.

Human pocket. Need me to carry anything? Don't worry, I've got plenty of pockets. In fact I'm all pockets: trouser pockets, coat pockets, front pockets, back pockets, inside pockets, outside pockets, breast pockets, ticket pockets. It's okay—bring that tiny bag just big enough for a lipstick and a mint; or better yet, no bag at all. I will carry your phone, your water, your glasses, your other glasses, your keys, your book. THAT'S WHY I WAS PUT ON THIS EARTH.

Once you start looking, there are all sorts of little ways you can make yourself useful. It's largely about being in the right place at the right time with the right skills. Above all, don't panic. It's probable that scare stories about male obsolescence are a trifle overstated. They said the same thing about the horse when the motor-car was invented, and you know what? I saw a horse just last week.

Married life does not, at first, seem much different to what went before. We don't argue less or more. We don't get any headed stationery. We don't behave more responsibly, or with a sense that people are expecting something new from us. When we bowl out of a party drunk at three a.m. and I turn to wave good-bye, only to turn back and find that my wife has completely disappeared, I do not regard her decision to ditch me as a marital impropriety, but simply a rotten thing to do. When I then hear a small voice saying "Help me" and realize that she has actually fallen over and become inextricably lodged in a hedge, I don't see it as being somehow incompatible with our vows. I just think about how hard it's going to be to get a taxi to stop for us if she's covered in leaves.

"I've lost a shoe in here," she says.

"Stop struggling," I say. "You're damaging the hedge."

Mostly, we are taking the time to enjoy being together without the imminent threat of having to break up. Eventually, however, things do begin to change. Speaking of my wife as "my wife" stops being funny—not that anyone ever laughed —and starts to seem oddly normal. The tiny flat is now full of wedding presents, many of which have a distinctly domestic agenda: You've got a flan dish, so when are you going to make some flan? I find myself in a position to open a current account. People ask us to dinner three weeks in advance, instead of three hours. I'm left notes in the morning reminding me to pick up the dry cleaning. From where? I think. Suddenly being married seems to come with an awful lot of stuff to do.

THE TWELVE LABORS OF MARRIAGE

Although there is an inevitable amount of sharing involved, a good marriage is, at its heart, an efficient division of labor. Couples in the first blush of love may go to Sainsbury's together, but they soon learn that this is a poor deployment of resources. Why should two people suffer? It makes far more sense to split the chores, especially those that are recurring and disagreeable. Certain dispiriting tasks can, by mutual agreement, be skipped completely. In our first two years of marriage neither my wife nor I did any ironing at all. Even today I only iron on a need-to-wear basis, and moments where I take off my jacket in public are invariably accompanied by the words "Yeah, sorry, I don't really do sleeves."

A key aspect of long-term compatibility is a complementary mix of domestic talents; ideally you each bring something to the table. But a finely honed skill usually reflects a corresponding belief in the importance of the chore in question—the things you're bad at tend to be the things you don't care about. For this reason too big a divergence of expertise can lead to disagreement about what to prioritize. Although it may leave you light on skills, in the long run you could do worse than marry someone who shares your position regarding the pointlessness of ironing. Ironing and drying up. Why make a chore out of the one thing dishes can do by themselves?

The division of labor is not an entirely satisfactory arrangement. There is nit-picking. There is cheating. There are inevitable imbalances— debts of labor run up and never repaid. Old skills atrophy from a lack of use because the relevant tasks have become someone else's problem. But you cannot, in the end, escape the Twelve Labors of Marriage. They must be negotiated, day in, day out, for as long as you both shall live.

Precisely how these labors are divided is a difficult question. One might simply split them —six apiece—but some are definitely more onerous than others. Certain tasks a single person must perform anyway—making the bed, say— are no more burdensome in a household of two; in other cases the workload doubles. A couple might choose to divide each labor in half—you do it one week, I'll do it the next—but this system doesn't take into account natural inclination or innate ability.

An equable division of labor is one of the main planks of successful partnership. For reference purposes, I can give you an idea how my wife and I split the Twelve Labors of Marriage. I'm not necessarily recommending that you do it our way. That is not what I am recommending at all.

1. *Social organization.* Unattractive as it may sound, in my marriage this chore is divided along rather traditional lines: my wife does all of it. She holds all the phone numbers and addresses, and she keeps me apprised of upcoming social events with only as much notice as is necessary. I have a diary of my own, but I don't really write in it, because it has no official status. Instead I just tell my wife about any bookings I may have accidentally made, and she either writes them down or cancels them.

Although I was never very good at organizing my social life, I was actually better at it twenty years ago, simply because back then I still had to do it. Now, in return for never having to plan anything ever, I'm more or less obliged to go where I'm told. I don't know if this is a good thing or a bad thing; I certainly don't miss having to make decisions, but I'm pretty certain that when you tell people you're going on holiday next week and they ask where, you're supposed to know the answer.

2. *Housework.* Most of the Twelve Labors of Marriage are divisible solely on the basis of either preference or talent, but not this one. Housework isn't cool, and nobody likes doing it. It requires no particular aptitude or bent. And you can't simply trade it for one of the other labors, because it's mammoth. An imbalance of responsibility for housework is one of the greatest causes of resentment between married couples, and my marriage is, in this regard, pretty typical. The only fair way to deal with housework, you might think, is to divide it up evenly.

Or perhaps not. There is a popular notion that housework should actually be assigned according to the economic theory of "comparative advantage." Simply put, this means that whichever of you can perform a task comparatively more efficiently should specialize in it, so long as this labor is effectively traded for another chore at which the other person excels. This way, less time overall is expended on housework, and both parties end up happier.

You might think that comparative advantage is the reason that women still end up doing most of the cleaning: because so many of them have the misfortune of being good at it. In the UK men still only manage about a third of the housework, and that's enough to put them at the top of the

87

European table. According to US Bureau of Labor statistics, 48 percent of American women, as opposed to just 20 percent of men, do housework on an average day.

You can blame the men, but you can't really blame comparative advantage, because that's not quite how it works. With comparative advantage it still makes sense for a husband to do the washing up even if he's the less efficient washer-upper, as long as there's another chore— mopping, let's say—at which he is so hopeless that there is a net gain of efficiency when he trades in one for the other.

The classic example used to demonstrate the benefits of comparative advantage, set forth by the economist David Ricardo in 1821, is the manufacture of wine and wool in Portugal and England. Portugal can make wine much more efficiently than England, so it makes sense to trade it for English wool, but even if Portugal can also produce wool more efficiently, it still makes sense to specialize in wine, as long as the comparative advantage in winemaking is bigger than the one for wool production.

There are a few problems with this system. You can be good at something and still really hate it —I can't imagine that being better at ironing would make me like it more—which means that the efficiency gained from chore specialization may not outweigh the accrued resentment. Male domestic inefficiency is often willful, and rarely reflects a genuine lack of aptitude. How long can you stay terrible at doing the washing up? Unless you're really trying not to, wouldn't you eventually get the hang of it? I'm living proof that through sheer dogged repetition a man can halve the time it takes him to put a cover on a duvet. Finally, comparative advantage cannot, by itself, erase the gender gap in housework. Maximum efficiency is not the same as fairness.

I did not, it must be said, bring a great number of comparative advantages to the domestic sphere. I'm perfectly willing to admit that I only do a third of the housework because, frankly, that statistic sounds a bit generous to me. What's even more shameful is that I'm home all the time, so any housework that is not done by me has to be done around me.

While I like to think I make a significant contribution, I don't imagine the Househusbands Union would be too kindly disposed toward my application. I only really use the Hoover after I've caused a catastrophic spill I don't want anyone to know about. There are certain forms of cleaning—dusting, for example—that I have never in my life engaged in. Like many men, my biggest contribution to housework reduction is that I've managed to lower the bar for cleanliness. But I'm glad I haven't had more influence here. I know what the house would look like if I were solely in charge of its cleaning. It would look like my office. My office looks like a compulsive hoarder's box room, the sort of place you might expect to find a skeleton in a bath-robe holding a copy of the *Radio Times* from December 2007.

Just remember what I said at the outset: this is not a self-help book. Do not be like me.

3. *Dealing with people who come to the door.* This is generally the task of whichever of you is foolish enough to open the door in the first place, but because I work from home, in our house it falls almost exclusively to me. In fact my entire daytime social circle is composed of Jehovah's Witnesses, fish sellers from Newcastle, postmen with packages for next door, charity muggers holding clipboards, and reformed criminals selling dustcloths.

I would like to be able to say that over the years I have developed a flair for deflecting a pushy sales pitch or being polite but firm with people who would attempt to save my immortal soul while my coffee gets cold. The truth is I am abrupt and susceptible by turns. I was once so compre-hensively dismissive of an ex-convict who wanted to charge me six quid for a lint roller that he was moved to shit on my doorstep, an act which doubtless set his rehabilitation back months. And yet I have also been known to agree to switch gas suppliers in order to get someone to go away before *Bargain Hunt* starts.

Even if I perform this particular labor brilliantly, I have nothing to show for it. When my wife comes home in the evening and asks me how my day was I do not say, "Today I dodged a freezer full of plaice and once again managed not to change broadband providers." But on those occa-sions when I am less than 100 percent successful, I am inevitably obliged to own up. "Today," I have to say, "I gave a con artist ten pounds for a sponsored walk he is never going to do, and then bought three months' worth of organic vegetable boxes from a pretty lady."

4. *Paperwork and administration.* It seems to me that this particular chore should be taken on by one person, because two people chipping in will only lead to confusion. But a marital home requires a preposterous amount of record-keeping, which is probably too much for one person to handle.

My wife rules over this sphere, because she's organized, although she lacks my ability to panic, and one of her chief organizational skills is throwing important paperwork away. I may be disorganized, but every bit of paper that has ever entered my office is still in there somewhere, and I can locate anything within a fortnight. In principle this mix of efficiency and hoarding should mean we're covered. In practice it means I shouted at her for binning a tax demand last week, and I've just found it under my desk.

5. *Cooking.* Some people possess both a talent for cooking and an ability to derive pleasure from exercising their skills to feed others. Whenever possible you should try to include such a person in your holiday plans, whether you enjoy that person's company or not.

But it's not uncommon to marry someone for love alone, even if that someone can't cook at all. My wife did, and so did I. Almost everything we know about cooking, we learned together, through a series of hideous culinary accidents.

Although I am normally reluctant to pass judgment on people's abilities or priorities, I will say this: not being able to cook is stupid. It just isn't that hard. You can even continue to dislike cooking, provided you learn to produce a palatable meal that can be thrown together using ingredients from the store cupboard or the corner shop in under an hour, and ends with the kitchen as clean as when you started. Then learn another one. Then learn . . . actually, two will probably do it, to be honest.

My wife and I pooled what little knowledge we had, and between us we developed a repertoire that spanned a seven-day meal cycle, if you included a takeaway on Sunday. These are not recipes as such, just dishes that have evolved over years of trial and error, including one which is simply called "Mexican" (it is not remotely Mexican, but it does call for four tins of refried beans), and a weird, paprika-tinged collection of odds and ends which in our house is known, with no great affection, as Spicy Ricey.* These two meals still remain in the rotation after fifteen years, but they are rarely served to outsiders.

Dinner parties are a different matter.

"I hate having dinner parties," says my wife.

"You're not supposed to say that while everyone's still here," I say, indicating our guests.

When we were first married there were only three requirements for a successful dinner party: a big ashtray, a bottle of wine per person, and a nearby shop that would sell you more wine after eleven p.m. The food was always, thankfully, an afterthought. Over the years, however, we grew weary of presenting meals we had to apologize for. We bought cookbooks, we took some culinary risks, and we learned to show off a little. At some

---

*Sweat one chopped onion, two finely chopped garlic cloves, one finely chopped chile (deseeded), one diced celery stalk, and one diced green pepper in a little olive oil. Add some scissored-up bacon if you have any. Tip in one and a half teaspoons sweet Spanish smoked paprika, a handful of frozen peas, two handfuls of those tiny frozen prawns, and a leftover chicken breast from lunch. From here you must choose one of two paths: my wife boils the rice separately and adds it after; I chuck it in dry—about a mugful—add water, stir, and put the lid on for ten minutes. Serves five people, as long as two of them don't really like it.

point I even discovered a recipe for chocolate éclairs shaped like swans, but I've only ever made them for people twice, and I was drunk both times. You have to be a bit drunk to think it's a good idea.

6. *Driving.* My wife and I have split this chore across national boundaries: when we're going somewhere in the car together, I drive only in America and on the Continent. The right side of the road is my domain. My wife is a very good driver, but she's not a great passenger; she refuses to accept that it is, by definition, a subordinate position. I, on the other hand, am an excellent passenger, which is just as well, because my wife has certain esthetic objections to my driving which she feels unable to keep to herself when I am at the wheel. This particular division of labor suits us both, although I am aware that it is unusual (apparently, when partners get in the car together, the man is four times more likely to drive) and I know that even if it doesn't feel particularly emasculating, it probably looks a little emasculating.

The only time I ever minded was on long car journeys with three children fighting in the back. As the free-handed passenger seat occupant, all in-car discipline fell to me, and as everybody with small children knows, there is no such thing as in-car discipline. Most of these trips adhered to a similar template:

"Make them stop fighting," says my wife.

"Right!" I say. "If you don't stop right now someone is getting out." It's my only in-car sanction—the out-car option. I've issued it countless times, without once following through on it. The only person I've ever met who actually left a child by the roadside was my mother.

"Dad is very angry," my wife says into the rearview mirror. "He's going to do something in a minute." The fighting does not even pause.

"Right," I say, wheeling round to point at the middle one. "You're getting out." He begins to laugh uncontrollably.

"Pull over," I say to my wife.

"I'm not pulling over," she says. "The traffic's only just started moving."

"If you want me to discipline them, you need to back up my hollow threats."

"We're late as it is," she says.

"I've run out of ideas," I say. "You discipline them."

"I can't," she says, "I'm driving." She's trying—preposterously—to make driving sound like the more unenviable chore. She might as well say, "I can't—I'm queuing for another go on the Ferris wheel."

"Pull over, and I'll drive," I say.

"Oh no, you won't," she says. The fighting in the back has turned nasty; the younger two are reaching across the older one to punch each other.

"Then pull over," I say, "and let me out here."

7. *Shutting down.* I am the person who runs through the nightly checklist that puts our house to bed: front door double-locked, front window bolted, old dog offered option of last-minute piss, garden door locked, lights out, taps closed, TV off, dishwasher on, fridge door shut, children asleep, kitchen demonstrably not on fire. It's not difficult, but it's a tremendous responsibility which I am pleased to assume. I only resent the reporting procedure that follows.

"Is the front door locked?" says my wife.

"Yes," I say.

"What about the garden door?"

"Yes," I say. It's good she has the checklist in her head, because she will have to take over the role if I die, but still.

"Are the children all asleep?"

"Yes," I lie.

"Are the lights in the kitchen . . ."

"I do all of these things," I say. "Every time."

"Except for last week, when you left two gas rings burning all night."

"That was not my fault," I say. "And I'll be right back."

8. *Standards enforcement.* At some point you must decide whether, as a marital unit, you comprise the sort of people who bother to put sugar in a bowl, or butter on a dish, or tea bags in a dedicated earthenware container that says

"TEA" on the front. You must set a standard for the lowest form of cheese allowed in your fridge, and an agreed method for making coffee. Do you care whether your car is clean, or do you use it as a mobile skip? Do you mind being a couple known for turning up late to everything? Are you minimalists? Are dogs allowed on your sofas? Is smoking allowed in your kitchen? Do you make people take their shoes off when they visit? Does a guitar on a stand count as furniture?

Our own standards—a loose mix of esthetic obstinacy, misguided principle, family tradition, resistance to change, latent snobbery, and squeamishness—were reached by consensus over a number of years, although enforcement is generally undertaken by the person who in each case actually gives a shit one way or the other. My wife is the one who makes sure there are no potted plants in the house. It is only at my insistence that we do not pour sugar into our tea straight from the bag, even though I don't take sugar, or tea.

From time to time household standards must be revised, either because of natural slippage, changes in taste, or a feeling that you've both reached an age where it's unacceptable to drink wine from old Nutella jars. Generally speaking, the fewer standards you can get away with maintaining, the better. After your tenth wedding anniversary, you should try to rid yourself of a couple every year.

9. *Finding things.* You may think the world is simply divided into finders and losers, but these roles are more often thrust upon us by the people we live with. I'm not a natural finder. It's only my wife's bottomless capacity to make stuff go missing that has forced me to become observant, methodical, and at ease going through the bins with a pair of Marigolds on. Most of all, I have become psychologically astute—you have to teach yourself to think like someone who wasn't thinking.

10. *Speaking to tradespersons.* This is my job, but it's not because I'm good at it. When I converse with plumbers or electricians I'm always desperate to make it sound as if I have a basic grounding in the mechanics of their profession. I never ask any pertinent questions, for fear of sounding stupid. Instead I nod grimly, misuse jargon, and offer my own fanciful suggestions regarding the nature of the problem, all of which contributes to making me a very easy person to rip off. My wife, on the other hand, makes no pretense of understanding anything. She treats the field of heating engineering as if it were a branch of witchcraft, and all its certified practitioners with naked suspicion. She really should take over the role, but she's almost never home when these people turn up.

11. *New stuff.* From time to time, while wrestling with a malfunctioning or outmoded kitchen tool, I will look up and say, with exasperation, "We really need a new one of these." I say this because it is not my job to decide that a new thing is required, or to secure that new thing. It's my wife's job. This is probably left over from the early days when she had all the money, but I have to come to accept that this responsibility should remain hers. I know how much regret a poor or unnecessary purchase can cause, and I want that regret to belong to someone else.

When it comes to the subject of buying replacement items—from potato peelers to sofa beds—I am like a lawyer arguing a case before a judge. If I do not prevail, then I may feel I have presented my case poorly, but ultimately it's not up to me. I don't mind. The stupider acquisitions that I argued so eloquently against—like the second dog—sit around all day serving as examples of what happens when my wisdom is not heeded. The stupid ones that I insisted upon, I hide.

12. *Nameless dread.* I retain sole charge of nameless dread: lying awake through the small hours, freaking out about things that haven't happened yet, but might. It's demanding and unrewarding, but if I didn't do it, it simply wouldn't get done.

In the tit-for-tat labor market of marital chores, nameless dread is a difficult commodity to trade. You can't get out of a trip to the supermarket by saying, "But I was up half the night worrying about interest rates!" It will be pointed out to you, again and again, that nameless dread is irrational and serves no earthly purpose. Some spouses will even go so far as to claim that it doesn't deserve its place among the Twelve Labors of Marriage, because it's really more of an illness. Such a spouse may even lobby for nameless dread to be supplanted in the list by DIY, in a bid to trick you into putting up some coat hooks.

But DIY is not one of the Twelve Labors of Marriage. DIY is a separate sphere, a territory that increasingly goes unclaimed by anyone. For the sake of your own continued relevance, mate, I'm going to suggest you make it your own.

6.

DIY: Man's Estate, Even Now

It is a function of our increasing dependence on technology that each new generation has a more tenuous connection with how stuff works. When my Wi-Fi starts performing poorly or patchily, I don't really understand the nature of the problem. I just resort to a sort of self-taught voodoo, wandering through the house with an iPad in search of a spot where the air is thicker with Internet.

You'd think that in such bewildering times we might seek refuge in the baldly mechanical, in nuts and bolts and nails and wire. In fact the age of the Internet should be a boom time for DIY—there are people out there whose only passion in life is posting online videos showing you how to change the drum belt on your tumble dryer—but it isn't.

DIY sales have been falling 4 or 5 percent a year on average, for a decade. And this lack of purchasing seems to be related to a general decline in skills. Surveys have shown that a majority of modern twentysomethings do not know how to change a fuse or unblock a drain.

Are they not embarrassed? Do they call in an electrician when they need a new plug fuse, or do they just buy a whole new toaster?

It would be marvelous if women were to achieve equal footing with men in the DIY department. It would be pretty good if we were even heading that way, but it's more likely that the sexes will only draw abreast on the downhill charge toward total incompetence. Men are losing their DIY skills, and women aren't taking up the slack. If you think ceding this ground has no consequences, think again. These days less than half of all adults—and only 17 percent of women—know how to change an automobile tire. One direct result of this national deskilling is that only about half of the new cars sold in the UK actually come with spare tires. It saves on cost and weight, and if nobody can put one on anyway, what's the point? By increments, your helplessness will be enshrined, and you will be left standing by the side of the road.

DIY may not be an inherently male thing, but it is sort of manly. Being handy remains a key component of What Women Want in a Man. Sensitivity is also good, but you can get away with being pretty emotionally stunted as long as you know how to put up a curtain rod. No one is suggesting you need to build an extension or reslate the roof, but at the very least you should be able to take the top off a toilet tank and not be surprised by what you find in there.

As a husband, you're not only in charge of all the DIY jobs your wife can't do, you're also in charge of the ones that you can't do either. You just have to learn how, because your wife will come to think less of you for not being able to fix a leaking tap. It's not her fault. It's the way she was raised.

You might say to yourself: Who cares what she thinks? As a man living through the End of Men, busy coming to terms with my own irrelevance —why should I bother with DIY now?

There are two reasons: first, I've already tested this excuse, and it doesn't go down very well at home; second—and you must imagine I'm whispering this—DIY is empowering. Competence is addictive. Contrary to what you may have been led to believe, life is not too short to countersink a screw.*

Getting to grips with DIY is not just a simple question of saving money, or making do instead of buying new. Actually, in many cases you'll find the economics are against you—replacement is often cheaper than repair. This is about taking control of your stuff, gaining a little mastery over your machines, and taking a hammer to

---

*The drilling of a shallow conical depression, using a drill fitting called a countersink, to allow a flat-headed screw to sit flush with the surface of the wood into which it is screwed. Since you ask.

the parts of your house that are pissing you off.

Like me, you may not be very good at DIY, but that just makes it all the more thrilling when things inexplicably go right. Don't worry about your lack of skill. One must proceed with the bold assumption that all there is to know about tiling is contained in the two-hundred-word instruction panel on the back of the tub of grout. Everything else comes from within.

Expertise is not your goal. You certainly don't want to get a local reputation for being good at stuff. Anyway, at its best, DIY is a voyage of self-discovery. For the professional installer, the laying of a rubber floor is not an epic fourteen-hour struggle of man versus glue. It's just another day at work. Personally, I lose interest in a DIY technique almost as soon as I've mastered it. That's why one of the cupboard doors under our stairs opens so smoothly, and the other still comes off in your hand. Repositioning hinges? Been there, done that, never again. But you know what? I just bought a new chisel and I'm keen to try it out. Show me something that needs gouging.

When embarking on a challenging repair job, never ask yourself, Will I make it worse? You cannot make the problem worse; you can only move it forward to a stage where professional intervention becomes urgently advisable. Bear in mind that before you started trying to fix it, it wasn't broken enough to justify a huge emergency call-out charge. Now it is. That's progress.

That said, there are some jobs where the risk/reward ratio makes ringing a qualified professional a better bet from the outset. Before you get stuck in a complex and daunting DIY project, run through this checklist of questions:

• Does the manual expressly forbid amateur installation or repair?

Show your spouse the relevant wording, and call the experts.

• Does the prospect of attempting it make you feel like crying?

It's not that you can't do it, but perhaps you're just not ready. If paying someone else to do it will make you stop crying, then it's probably money well spent.

• Has the object in need of repair presently got flames shooting out of the back of it?

Strictly speaking, that's one for the fire brigade.

• Are you missing a necessary tool that costs more than £100?

A DIY project should not be an excuse for reckless shopping. Of course, once you've got your own personal diesel-powered compaction plate, you may end up using it all the time.

- Is it one of those jobs that requires you to know where hidden pipes/wires are/aren't?

These days pipes and wires are installed at a depth beyond the reach of the average shelf screw, but you do not want to find out the hard way that yours aren't.

- How high off the ground is the site of the problem? Would you die if you fell from there?

Before we got satellite TV, one of my regular maintenance jobs involved climbing out of a second-floor window and hauling myself onto the flat roof at the back of the house in order to whack the aerial back into position with a mop handle. Looking up there now, I honestly do not know what I was thinking.

- Is the cause of the trouble so baffling to you that you suspect poltergeists?

This has happened to me twice: once when it started raining in the sitting room, and once when the burglar alarm started going off whenever the phone rang. In the latter case, I didn't even know what sort of repairman to call. I thought about ringing a priest.

I was not born to this work.
My first adventures in DIY involved standing or

lying alongside my father as he tackled small repair jobs. Although a dentist by training, he did not fear basic plumbing, routine engine maintenance, hard landscaping, or simple carpentry. He could gap a spark plug, patch a driveway, or plant a fence post—jobs I have never had occasion to attempt. He did not, in any formal sense, teach me anything about DIY, but I learned a lot about swearing. He also instilled in me the belief that in most cases it was worth having a go, and he once showed me how to mold a missing lawnmower part from the stuff they make dentures out of.

It is a tradition I have carried on with my sons. I never undertake a big DIY job without first tracking down a child to hold my tools.

"Why me?" the child always screams.

"Because I found you first," I say. "Bad luck."

Usually I preface the task with a short lecture—an overview of the problem, and my proposed solution, right or wrong—before moving on to step-by-step narration.

"So by turning the valves on either side to the twelve-o'clock position," I say, "I isolate the filter from the system, enabling me to remove the bottom portion. Or so says YouTube."

"And why I am here?" says the boy.

"You are here because insurance companies like witnesses."

"But it's boring," he says.

"Boring is good," I say. "Trust me—we do not want this to become in any way interesting."

"If you say so."

"Hold the torch higher."

"I am."

"Christing fuck, where is all this water coming from?"

Not many skills are passed on in these sessions—they're mostly small lessons in coping with humiliation—but I feel the need to show my sons that sometimes a determined incompetence is all it takes to get the job done. You need no special gifts beyond a certain patience with your own uselessness.

When I was their age I possessed as few skills as they do, although I eventually became adept at fixing the things that broke in our house most often. I could fit a new screen into a door blindfolded, because the dog burst through our screens on a weekly basis in summer and my mother took to buying replacement screening in big rolls to keep up with the damage. The job even came with its own special tool—a spline roller, it was called—which I wielded with considerable aplomb. But my knowledge remained local and specific, with large gaps in my understanding.

Later, as a renter specializing in arrears, I never had much use for DIY. Repairs were just something various landlords refused to take care of until I paid up or moved out. My DIY career didn't really get started until I moved to Britain.

During my first summer in London I have nothing to do while the world works all day. I spend the idle hours watching cricket on telly, but it would be fair to say I don't understand the game—I can't even tell whether they're playing or just waiting to play. My girlfriend has recently moved into a one-bedroom flat in a newly refurbished terrace. Or mostly refurbished—the kitchen floor is still bare plywood. In a rash moment, during a touchy conversation about finances, I offer to install whatever sort of flooring she wants.

One day she comes home with a single square ceramic tile—French, provincial, roughly cast, and about a centimeter thick. I cannot imagine how one would go about making it stick to the floor, but I am outwardly resolute.

"I can do this," I say. "Easy." I'm not actually certain I can do it, but how hard can it be? They're floor tiles, not ceiling tiles. Gravity will be on my side.

The tiles are ordered. Only when they arrive do I realize I can't cut them; they're too thick. I can barely smash them with a hammer. Someone tells me I need a wet saw. I pretend to know what that is.

A wet saw, I soon discover, is a high-speed circular saw with a water trough at the bottom to keep the diamond cutting blade from overheating. It is not the sort of thing the amateur floor tiler owns. It is the sort of thing he hires.

I do not possess the credentials required to rent anything in the UK. I don't have a credit card or a bank account or, strictly speaking, an address. I don't even know the words one would use to negotiate such a transaction in Britain. My girlfriend, I decide, must hire a wet saw for me. In terms of personal emasculation, this is a memorable low point. I go with her to the hire shop but insist on lurking at the back, pretending to be another customer.

"Hello, I would like to hire a wet saw, please," she says to the man behind the counter. He is wearing a long brown coat, and a smirk.

"What do you want with a wet saw?" he says, using the special patronizing tone men in brown coats reserve for women.

"I'm not telling you," she says.

"If you don't know what you want it for, how d'you know you need one?" he says.

"It's none of your business why I want it," she says. "Perhaps I'll take two."

This goes on for half an hour, during which period I feel the need to leave the shop and wait outside. By the time I return she has secured the wet saw, but she is refusing to let the man take her picture with a camera mounted above the till. He keeps pushing the button, and she keeps ducking.

Eventually we get the wet saw home, but it's not until the next morning that I have an opportunity to be alone with it. My standing in the eyes of my English girlfriend is at stake; I have made it sound as if expertise in these matters is something they hand out to everyone in America, and that I am a fairly typical representative of a highly competent super-race. Privately I'm just hoping the instructions will make everything clear, but there are no instructions apart from a sticker warning me not to cut my hand off.

It sure slices tiles, though—quickly, easily and, once I get the hang of it, quite accurately. It's incredibly loud and spews dust into the air, but I get all my cutting done by the afternoon, and am ready to start sticking the tiles to the floor. This is when I realize there's a reason people are paid for this sort of work. It's messy, awkward, and very hard on the knees. The walls aren't straight, and the floor isn't quite level. The next morning I discover that only about 30 percent of the tiles have stayed stuck. I chip all the old grout off the backs of the others and stick them down again. The next day 50 percent of those tiles have come up, plus 10 percent of the original 30 percent of stuck ones. When my girlfriend is home, I act as if this is to be expected, maintaining a cloudy aura of confidence in my work so far, as if belief itself might hold some more of these tiles to the fucking floor.

It takes a week before all the tiles stay put when you walk on them. If it were my job I'd have got fired on day two, but I consider it a triumph.

Haltingly, I begin to get to grips with being the person in our relationship who's in charge of whatever needs doing in the DIY line. But it's not easy—moving countries means that what little jargon I ever understood is now a foreign language. I don't know the word English people use when they want to buy spackle. In the UK they say "paraffin" for "kerosene," have two kinds of lightbulb fittings, and don't always understand what the word "Phillips" means when applied to the head of a screwdriver. Everything is measured in metric; every fixing and fastening is a mystery. Few of my native skills prove to be of any use. In twenty years in the UK I have never come across a screen door that needs mending.

Fortunately my arrival on these shores coincides with the rise of the DIY superstore. Within a couple of years they are everywhere. Never again do I have to endure a patronizing exchange with a man behind a counter who wants to know precisely what type of hinge I need, while I pretend to know what types of hinges there are.

Now I can just go to the Homebase hinge aisle and buy a whole range—flush hinges, butt hinges, strap hinges, exposed, concealed, cranked, torque, levered, self-closing—without having to discuss it with anyone. One of them is bound to be right, and the others can sit in the tool cupboard awaiting future hinge challenges. It is one of the luxuries of long-term marital commitment that you can buy DIY materials without having a specific project in mind. Each purchase is a tiny act of faith that says, "I will still be here when whatever this thing is supposed to fix finally breaks."

But a lack of tools is one of the most difficult aspects of being new to DIY—you can't get very far without the right gear. Trying to kit yourself out from scratch is expensive and potentially wasteful. You don't want any tools you can't operate, or ones designed for tasks you are unlikely to encounter in your lifetime. However much you think you want it, don't buy a router, not even in a sale.

You will, however, need a few key things to get started. Thankfully you won't even have to go to a big-box superstore for most of this stuff—you should be able to pick it up in any decent corner shop.

THE BEGINNER'S ESSENTIAL DIY TOOL CUPBOARD

Glue. There are lots of types of glue, but you only need one kind: epoxy resin. This is the sort that comes in two tubes that you have to mix together. It takes a long time to set, but anything you stick together with this stuff stays stuck. All other glues are, frankly, a waste of time. Epoxy resin is also an essential form of replacement matter—you can build up broken edges with it, or reconstruct small parts by carving hardened globs of it. It's a vital tool in the repair of cheap plastic toys.

Clamps. This is to clamp things you've glued, so you don't have to hold them together with your fingers for twelve hours. You'll need several sizes.

A random assortment of "making good" materials. There are many different plasters, putties, primers, fillers, mortars, hardeners, and sealants out there, designed to patch all manner of cracks and holes, or to render surfaces smooth, sound, and paintable. They're not meant to be interchangeable, but they sort of are.

A vise-grip. It's like an adjustable, sprung grabber that locks on to things with tremendous tenacity, and replaces virtually all wrenches. Also counts as part of your clamp collection.

Duct tape. Strong, sticky, and rippable into custom lengths, duct tape is a brilliant temporary solution—and a pretty good permanent solution—for most of life's problems. I find it especially useful for securely affixing vacuum cleaner attachments that belong to an altogether different vacuum cleaner. Also counts as part of your clamp collection.

An electric drill. Just as you can't make an

omelet without breaking eggs, you can't DIY without putting holes in things.

A comprehensive set of screwdrivers. There aren't just two kinds of screwdriver. There are about forty. When manufacturers don't want you fixing their products yourself, they often put them together using screws with peculiar heads—star-shaped, hexagonal, etc.—in the hopes that you won't have the screwdriver to match. This effrontery is reason enough to have one of every kind there is. Anything you own, you should be able to take to bits, unless you own an X-ray machine.

A scraper thing. Or a putty knife, if you like technical jargon. Mostly used to jam filler into cracks or to remove old paint. Also counts as part of your screwdriver collection.

Reading glasses. If you need them, you will need them.

A selection of sandpapers. From the sort so rough that it hurts to pick it up, to one so smooth you can't tell which side is the back, and a few in between.

A selection of wall plugs, with screws to match. Were it not for John Joseph Rawlings, your house would have no curtain rods, wall mirrors, or loo roll holders. All but your smallest pictures would be sitting on the floor, and your overhead lights would be hanging from their wires.

Rawlings foresaw this nightmarish vision over a

century ago, and patented the Rawlplug. Before that the method for fixing things to masonry was complicated, time-consuming, and beyond the limited skills of the average householder. His original plug was a jute fiber tube held together with glue and animal blood, but it worked on the same principles as today's plastic equivalent: you drill a hole of appropriate size, tap in the plug, and then drive a screw into its center. As you turn the screw the plug deforms outward, expanding to fill the space and provide grip.

A bag of plastic cable ties. First developed in the 1950s by the US electrical company Thomas & Betts, the cable tie—or zip tie—has become the great quick fix of modern times. This simple ratcheted plastic loop can be used to lash any-thing to anything—you just pull it tight with a pair of pliers and it stays tight until you cut it off. Very good for sticking bits of your car back on.

IKEA tools. Hang on to those funny one-off tools that come with flat-pack purchases, in case you need to take the furniture in question apart later. When you build a child's cot in situ, there's never any compelling reason to check whether the completed unit will fit through the door. It won't.

Random broken stuff. Every blown light fitting, redundant switch plate, or bent handle you replace will contain a screw, nut, washer, or spring that might be useful for fixing something else later on. You need to store all these small parts in old jars and unlabeled envelopes. To be honest, these pieces of saved junk rarely come in handy, but the bits you throw away are always the ones you'll wish you'd kept. A growing array of useless hardware inevitably leads to disputes about cupboard space, which is probably why my entire collection disappears every eighteen months or so.

There. You're ready for 75 percent of the DIY challenges you're likely to face this year, and you haven't even bought a saw yet.

Obviously, when you wish to pick up a new skill late in life in a desperate bid to shore up your self-worth, you don't start with the basics. If you wanted to learn to play the guitar in a hurry, you wouldn't begin with the correct posture, some fingering exercises, a lesson on musical notation, and a series of simple scales. You'd just go up to someone who can already play the guitar and say, "Show me the easiest song there is." In that same tradition of the quick fix, we'll jump straight into DIY at the shallow end, headfirst, without looking.

FIVE THINGS YOU CAN ACTUALLY FIX BY HITTING THEM WITH A HAMMER

1. *Central heating pump.* Sometimes gunk or scale from the system travels up to the pump and blocks it—think of it as your house experiencing

a cardiac event. A judicious thump with a nicely weighted hammer can sometimes jerk the blockage free. I've done it myself, although not successfully. In the end I had to pay a plumber to come out and hit the pump slightly harder.

2. *Car starter.* On those occasions when you turn the key in the ignition and nothing happens, it's often worth opening the hood and giving the starter motor a considered tap, which can loosen the stuck mechanism, or allow the worn-out brushes to make contact, or something. I've tried this technique using a tent peg hammer from Millets, and it worked perfectly, although I should say I wasn't entirely certain which bit was the starter motor—even after I printed out a picture of one—so I ended up hitting a lot of things for good measure.

3. *Recalcitrant flat tire.* Let's say, for the sake of argument, that you've got as far as removing the lug nuts and you've already jacked up the car, and yet the wheel still won't come off—it's jammed on there from driving. A sharp blow from the biggest hammer you own should knock it from its housing. Alternatively, you could try kicking it. If the car falls off the jack, you're doing it too hard.

4. *Unsound plaster/render analysis.* How extensive is the problem? There's one easy way to find out: just keep hitting it until it stops falling off. I should probably point out that this is just step one in a rather involved repair project.

5. *Virus-plagued computer.* Admittedly drastic, and certainly a measure of last resort—but foolproof. Also very satisfying.

THE THREE EASIEST
DIY JOBS THERE ARE

1. *Replace your windscreen wipers.* In terms of improving your outlook, both metaphorically and actually, you will find no better investment than new wipers. Up until quite recently, if you'd told me that windscreen wipers were expensive and difficult to fit, or were specific to your car model, or could only be removed using a special tool you needed a certificate to own, I would have believed you. It turns out wipers are universally adaptable, simple to install, and the poshest pair you can buy will only set you back about thirty quid. I don't want to put ideas in your head, but they're so easy to unclip that you could just steal a pair from another car. Here's something else you may never have noticed, because you spend so much time staring through them instead of at them: the driver's-side wiper is considerably longer.

2. *Fix inadequate rinse cycle.*

The problem: When you pull them hot from the dishwasher, some, if not all, of your dishes and glasses are encrusted with unidentifiable matter. This could be caused by some complex plumbing or software problem, but more often than not it's because small bits of detritus are blocking the water-jet holes in the spinning spray arms, so they don't turn, and if they don't turn, they don't rinse. In theory the culprit could be anything small enough to work its way into the intake, but big enough to block the holes, but in practice it's almost always either pine nuts or Puy lentils. It is, truly, a middle-class curse.

The solution: The spray arms—there are two, upper and lower—detach easily. Just run water through them under the tap and shake them out over the sink until whatever is caught in there falls out, and replace. I once wrote a book where the main character performed this simple act of maintenance, and I got an e-mail from a reader who said I'd saved him £250. It's still the best review I've ever had.

3. *Broken toilet handle.* The mechanics inside the average toilet tank are agreeably primitive: flicking the handle yanks up a plunger, releasing the stored water into the bowl. The plunger then falls back into place, and the tank refills until a floating ball on a stick rises high enough to shut off the valve.

The most common problem you'll face is the handle becoming detached from the plunger. They may have been connected by a length of wire which has rusted through, or by a chain that has decoupled. Anything of adjustable length and sufficient sturdiness (a cable tie, for example) will serve as a replacement. Mine is presently hooked together with an E string from a guitar.

From this point, with these meager skills, you can take DIY as far as you please. You can start building Shaker furniture, or, like me, you can remain the sort of barely skilled person who is not afraid to pull apart a malfunctioning Xbox controller, on the grounds that the problem might just be a loose spring, and you will be a complete hero if you can get it working again. If you can't, it was always going to end up in the bin anyway.

And you know what? Eventually, through experience and practice, you get better at DIY. As long as the trial and error doesn't kill you (Have you turned off the electricity?), some of these jobs can even begin to seem like routine maintenance, i.e., boring. But there is no satisfaction quite like standing under a formerly malfunctioning light fitting while switching it on and off and explaining in some detail to your wife what exactly was wrong and how you—in the face of considerable adversity, and using a butter knife for a screwdriver because you couldn't find one thin enough—managed to put it right.

Each DIY project successfully completed constitutes a small personal triumph that sits in your house like a trophy in a case. I could take you on a tour of mine. Look at this skylight shade—I had to replace the old broken one, which was not, I can tell you, a simple matter.

Now this one is broken too, but that's because people are always pulling on it too hard. See the new tiles around the edge of the shower? I did those—straight or what? In the right light you can't even tell they don't match the old ones. Who knew there was more than one kind of white?

Come downstairs. Notice how the phone extension wire hugs the skirting board? Not as easy as it looks. Check out the way this sink drains—quite slowly, I'll admit, but you should have seen it before. And look up, up to the ceiling, to the brown, Australia-shaped stain caused by a leaking toilet tank; a stain which, thanks to my timely intervention and a huge blob of sealant, hasn't got any bigger since 2006. I'm the one who drew the pencil outline round it to prove it.

7.

Extended Family

I am sitting in a restaurant with my wife and my mother-in-law. They are busy making calculations on some paper napkins—calculations having to do with money—and I am keeping very quiet. Without warning, they both turn and look at me. It must have something to do with the expression on my face.

"Don't worry," says my wife. "We're only going to do this if it's what you want to do."

"I'm cool," I say, refilling my wineglass.

I have already decided that it would not do for me to have strong views on the matter. For a start, none of the money being transferred from napkin A to napkin B is mine. I would incur no financial risk as a result of what's being proposed.

Here is what's being proposed: my wife sells her one-bedroom flat, my mother-in-law sells her home in Wiltshire, and we use the money to buy a house in London, a house substantial enough that we can all live in it together comfortably.

There are several reasons why this is a good idea. My mother-in-law has medical reasons for wishing to be in the capital. My wife and I, mean-while, are looking for more living space, but are reluctant to move toward the fringes of London in order to get it. The One Big House plan provides an efficient solution to several problems, a solution so blatantly traditional that it seems almost modern. My wife and her mother are acting as if they invented it.

There are also some reasons why it is a bad idea. My wife and her mother have a close but slightly intense relationship. Much of the time they get along famously, but I have seen them shriek at each other for entire weekends, and I find it awkward being in the middle. I accept that I am part of the family now, but maybe not this much.

Secretly, I harbor only the strongest of reservations. I believe that a good working relationship with one's mother-in-law requires a certain distance, and I can't imagine her opinion of me will be improved by proximity. Even at thirty I feel a bit young to enter into an arrangement that strikes me as being both emotionally and financially irreversible—if we all move in together, it will be permanent.

It's not exactly a dilemma I'm facing. I can sense that my marriage depends on my responding to the plan in the right way, and I am prepared to endorse the proposal wholeheartedly, which is why offering an actual opinion at this point would be a waste of everybody's time. In any case I'm fairly certain the scheme will never get off the ground. For the kind of money they're spending, in the kind of neighborhoods they're looking, I'm betting there is no such house.

I'm wrong. Not only is there such a house, there is one less than a mile from the flat. And not only is it on the market, it is languishing on the market. The price has just been dropped because the owners are desperate to return to Australia. Before I really know what's happening I find myself standing in its cavernous sitting room, surrounded by boxes.

Not all our friends think this is such a great idea. To some it sounds a retrograde step, or a forward leap toward social ossification. Maybe they think there's something a bit Edwardian about it, or that they'll have to keep their voices down when they come over. I find myself in the odd position of having to defend the project.

"Look," I tell them. "It's really two entirely separate dwellings. We just happen to share a front door."

But there is work to be done on that front: before our flat can be self-contained and self-sustaining, we need to convert the attic into a bedroom, and one of the bedrooms into a small kitchen. Work progresses slowly, but by winter we're all moved in, and there seems to be plenty of space. If my wife and her mother choose to argue, I can simply remain upstairs, out of sight and out of earshot.

In February my wife goes away for work for

three days. It is the first time my mother-in-law and I have been alone in the house together, and I am unsure of the etiquette. When I get home that evening I slip quietly up the stairs to our dusty, half-built kitchen. I have a vague plan for a mean little meal and an early night, but there is no food, so I will have to slip quietly back down the stairs to go to the shops, and quietly back up them again. I sit in the gathering gloom for a while, preparing to make my move.

The phone rings. It is my mother-in-law, calling from downstairs.

"What are your plans for supper?" she says.

"I don't really, I hadn't . . ."

"I have lamb," she says.

The Winter Olympics has just started, so we sit in her kitchen eating lamb, drinking a bottle and a half of wine, and watching the figure skating on a portable telly. It's the pairs compulsory.

"It's rather amazing, isn't it?" she says.

"Absolutely," I say.

On the second night my mother-in-law rings again.

"I bought a chicken from the butcher," she says. We watch the individual routines.

On the third night I feel as if I ought to give my mother-in-law a break from cooking for me—not least because my wife is due home and I don't want to get caught sponging—but she rings again, right on time.

"It's only spaghetti, I'm afraid," she says. "But it's also the pairs long routine."

My wife arrives home in the middle of supper; she's had a difficult few days filming on location, and she's in a corresponding mood. She drops her bag and sits down between us.

"Why are you watching this?" she says.

"It's the pairs final," her mother says.

"I hate fucking figure skating," says my wife, "and so do you."

"Actually," says my mother-in-law, looking at me, "we find it rather fascinating." My wife turns to look at me.

"No, you don't," she says.

"He loves it," says my mother-in-law. I find myself on weird and dangerous ground. I've never had to commit to an opinion about figure skating before. On the one hand, I agree: it's preposterous. If I were alone in my own kitchen, I'd be watching something else. But I've built up an unprecedented three-day rapport with my mother-in-law based entirely on its intricacies. To disavow figure skating now would be both disloyal and disastrous. Also, I've invested a lot of emotion in this pairs final.

"No comment," I say. "Would you excuse me?" I go to the loo and sit there quietly for a bit, in the hope that my absence will draw some of the heat from the situation. At this point I realize my new living situation will oblige me to draw on reserves of a quality I happen to possess in abundance: spinelessness.

When I return to the table three minutes later, I find the pair of them holding handfuls of spaghetti over each other's heads.

"Well, this has escalated," I say.

"If you don't accept that figure skating is interesting," my mother-in-law says, "I'm going to put this spaghetti on your head."

"If you don't say figure skating is stupid," says my wife, "I'm going to put this spaghetti on your head."

"Did you take that from my plate?" I say. "I wasn't finished."

The standoff continues. I decide not to intervene, curious to see how this sort of thing resolves itself. Eventually my wife reaches up and pokes her mother's spaghetti hand with the tines of her fork. My mother-in-law drops the spaghetti. She squeezes the back of her hand until four little red dots appear.

"I'm going to show this to your sister," she says.

8.

The Forty Guiding Principles of Gross Marital Happiness

Successful cohabitation requires a couple to address many disparate and competing aims, but it may help to think of your overall strategy as being analogous to Bhutan's mandated objective of Gross National Happiness. First proposed by the fourth Dragon King of Bhutan in 1972, the concept of Gross National Happiness alloyed living standards, physical and spiritual well-being, environmental impact, and stability to develop an index to measure the nation's progress. And it works pretty well in Bhutan (the land of Gross National Happiness), as long as you're not a member of the 20 percent of the population—mainly Hindus of Nepali origin—who were expelled from the country in the 1990s.

In marriage you and your partner must work together to construct a domestic operation that will make both of you as happy as possible without sacrificing the collective health, security, or long-term stability of the partnership. I realize that put that way it sounds boring, which is precisely why I coined the catchy term Gross Marital Happiness.

When I said this wasn't a self-help book, that was because everything I know about staying married can be boiled down to forty pretty basic insights. Actually, only thirty-nine—three of these are bollocks—but I wanted a round number.

1. Go to bed angry if you want to. It is often said that a couple should never let the sun set on an argument, but this isn't practical. Some arguments are, by their nature, two-day events: too much is at stake to set an arbitrary bedtime deadline. Faced with a stark choice between closure and a night's sleep, you're better off with the latter in almost every case. I've gone to bed angry loads of times, with no particular deleterious effects. You don't actually stay angry. It's a bit like going to bed drunk; you wake up feeling completely different, if not necessarily better.

2. Not liking cats isn't really a good enough reason to put your foot down. You have to be properly allergic, or weirdly phobic.

3. Marriages and other long-term relationships have a significant public element. Like an iceberg, the bulk of a marriage is hidden from view, but the top bit, the bit that you take out to parties and show off, should appear exemplary to outsiders: charming without being cloying; happy without being giddy; entertainingly spiky, but also mutually respectful. Above all, the whole thing should look effortless. Everybody knows

marriage is hard. No one wants to watch you do the work.

4. The question of whether a woman should adopt her husband's surname after marriage (or whether some double-barreled compound is preferable) is politically freighted, but what no one tells you before marriage is that changing your name is a huge drag. You'll need to pay for a new passport (£72) and you can be fined for driving on your old license. You'll have to inform your bank, your employer, HMRC, the insurance company, PayPal, and the Nectar card people. You'll need to take your marriage certificate to the bank to cash checks in your old name. Complications resulting from the switch will plague you for years afterward. And the benefits? There are no benefits. It's a complete waste of time. Forget principle and tradition: refuse to change your name on the grounds that you can't be arsed.

5. Even a marriage with healthy levels of communication can't make a dent in the huge stockpile of things that simply never get said. If the pair of you spent all day every day trying to express what's in your soggy little hearts, you'd never manage to get through a box set together. For purely practical reasons certain of your partner's desires, ambitions, and motivations will have to be guessed at. You should also learn to become an efficient curator of your own inner life:

display the important stuff, shove the rest in storage, and rotate occasionally to keep things interesting.

6. The time-honored debate about leaving the loo seat up or down is not a genuine source of friction in marriage; only between roommates who don't like each other anyway. The real rule, simple and inarguable, is this: don't piss on the seat. If you have sons, it is your sworn duty as a father to impress the importance of this rule upon them. When it comes to maintaining a happy marriage, I can't tell you what my failure to do so has cost me.

7. The marital bond is also a kind of codependency. The stronger your marriage, the harder it is to refrain from alcohol for two days a week if one of you thinks it's a stupid idea. It's rather sweet that you feel your spouse's refusal to join in amounts to permission for you to backslide, but it's not good for you.

8. When your wife carries on the next morning as if yesterday's argument never happened, you should interpret her behavior as a willingness to forgive and forget, and not as a sign that she actually has forgotten. The benefit of the doubt is a key aspect of Gross Marital Happiness, and even if she has forgotten there is nothing to be gained from guessing right.

9. If there is a single, immutable difference between men and women, it's that women will

almost never pretend they didn't see a heap of cat sick on the stairs.

10. Or at least I used to think so. It turns out anyone can learn this tactic, and quickly become better at it than you.

11. Think of the work of your relationship less as negotiation, and more as navigation. Marriage isn't an ongoing dispute to be settled; it's a lifelong course to be plotted. Also, you should really try to enjoy the journey, because the destination sucks.

12. When it comes to questions such as "How do I look in this?" "Do sideburns suit me?" "Are these trousers all right?" and "Do you like my new hair?" everyone, male or female, appreciates something that sounds like an honest answer. This is not necessarily the same as an honest answer.

13. There is no good rejoinder to the exclamation "I am NOT your mother!" but among the especially not good ones is "Then stop buying me ugly sweaters!" Take my word for it.

14. Spending time together is an important component of Gross Marital Happiness, but it shouldn't seem important; you don't want to feel undue pressure to enjoy yourselves. One of the most solemn promises I have made to my wife is that I will never, ever take her on a minibreak.

Doing normal, everyday things as a couple counts as relationship maintenance, in the same way that housework counts as exercise. Walking the dog counts. Eating breakfast together counts. Wandering aimlessly through a deserted shopping precinct together counts. Watching TV together doesn't count, unfortunately, although I'm currently appealing this.

15. One of the easiest ways to make a spouse feel needed is to seek their counsel on a particular subject, as if your spouse were your line manager. Remember: you're just after a bit of guidance or wisdom. Don't present yourself as a mess to be cleaned up, which you also shouldn't do with your line manager.

16. Buy the second-biggest bed you can afford. Even if you are now happy sleeping stacked like cordwood in what is known as a "small double" (that's four feet across), you should think about acquiring a future-proof mattress, one that can accommodate many nights of going to bed angry, strange new sleeping positions aimed at alleviating back or shoulder pain, a six- to eight-year interval in which at least one child with nits is in your bed at all times, and a late middle period where the strict rule you made about dogs on the bed breaks down. The reason you should buy the *second*-biggest bed you can afford is so you know there's one remaining upgrade available in case of emergency. I occasionally price up a "European super king" (6′6″ × 6′6″), which would enable my wife and me to sleep in a

T formation. I'll probably never buy it, but I'm glad it's out there.

17. Postal etiquette is important. If an envelope is not addressed to you, you shouldn't open it unless you have been expressly instructed to do so for the purpose of reading its contents out loud over the phone. This includes any envelope addressed, ironically or otherwise, in the old-fashioned style of "Mrs. [Your Male Christian Name, Followed by Shared Surname]," although on these occasions you can always claim to have made an honest mistake ("I thought it was meant for me!"). Exceptions to this rule include any catalog you might wish to peruse over lunch.

If an envelope is addressed to both of you, it's fair game, even if your name comes second. Whenever you receive exciting or scary post—test results, medical or academic; stark-looking letters from the bank; very large checks—it's considered good form to wait and open it together.

18. It's okay to steal small amounts of money from one another. Under most circumstances it's acceptable to liberate cash from the pockets/ wallet/purse of your other half while he/she sleeps or is elsewhere. The ready cash that exists in your home at any given time is a form of joint savings account, and there is a maximum amount that may be withdrawn without permission or explanation. That figure may need to be adjusted

for inflation occasionally, but at the time of writing it's £10.

19. Sharing can be ugly. People misplace stuff, forget stuff, run out of stuff, and neglect to buy stuff—it's human—and in cases where you possess an identical or perfectly serviceable equivalent, you should not be difficult about handing it over to your spouse on request. This includes, but is by no means limited to, travel cards, bank cards, house keys, car keys, your mobile phone, a razor (male to female only, and don't ask for it back; you don't want it), your deodorant, and yes, on occasion, your toothbrush. You should fully expect your selflessness to be reciprocated in your time of need, even if it isn't.

20. A spouse's appalling taste in music must be pardoned, since any effort to improve it is doomed to fail. If you think your spouse's musical taste is appalling, chances are she doesn't think much of yours either.

21. If you don't have someone other than your spouse—a friend, sibling, or colleague—that you can go to a movie with at short notice, you will end up seeing only about half the movies you wanted to see before you die.

22. It is generally acknowledged that a cheap appliance is a false economy, destined to cast a pall of impermanence over your household. But the opposite is true of toasters. The cost of a toaster is in inverse proportion to the quality of toast it

produces, and pricier models tend to be less robust, and are responsible for much unnecessary marital discord. A posh toaster is a false extravagance.

23. Never go out on Valentine's Day. As far as relationships go, February 14 is amateur night. Book a table for the thirteenth instead; you'll have the restaurant to yourselves.

24. Remember: marriage isn't all good. Like anything ultimately beneficial, marriage has some unwanted side effects. It can leave participants feeling hemmed in, held back, and harried. It represents an ongoing threat to one's individuality, personal privacy, fulfillment, and freedom. You will be happier once you understand that this works both ways. When you're feeling resentment, for example, it helps to bear in mind that you are also, at some level, resented.

25. Early on in marriage it's vital for a couple to agree upon an easily recognizable gesture—a raised eyebrow, say, or a discreetly pointed elbow—that will henceforth serve to mean "You see this person I am talking to? Please use his name in a sentence immediately. I have forgotten it."

26. Naturally there is a lot of disagreement in any partnership, but make certain you're on the same side when battling outside forces: unfeeling authority, intractable bureaucracy, strangers who have parked stupidly. Mindless solidarity is vital

under these circumstances—fight side by side, or run away together giggling, but don't be divided. Occasionally this them-against-us attitude can lead to couples resorting to criminal behavior—like Bonnie and Clyde—but even that can be very cementing, and you know what? I'm not a cop.

27. Love is one of those emotions you occasionally have to talk yourself into. In the teeth of the shit storm of accusation and recrimination that marriage can sometimes turn into, it's vital you take time out to dwell upon all the things about your partner that are admirable, exceptional, and charming. Sometimes it's easier to do this when your partner is asleep.

28. Own your stupidity. Self-awareness is a reliably endearing trait, and over time your spouse will come to admire your willingness to recognize precisely when you have been/are being an idiot. In fact an objective grasp of your own stupidity is almost preferable to not being stupid in the first place, and it's much, much easier.

29. Being married is like sharing a basement with a fellow hostage: after five years there are very few off-putting things you won't know about one another. After ten years there are none. Don't worry too much about having revealed yourself over time to be a weak, irritating, and physically disgusting human being—the trick is to maintain a daily standard consistently above your most

unattractive self. Once your partner has seen you at your worst, she'll realize how much effort you're putting in just to make yourself presentable.

30. As a periodic experiment, try pretending that everything your partner says during an argument is factually correct. It's easy to be a good listener—you just close your mouth and sit on your hands—but it can be difficult to see other people's opinions the way they do—as the truth—especially when they are wrong.

31. When it comes to marriage, there is no such thing as a false sense of security. There is only security and its opposite, and nothing stays the same for long. Stop worrying that your feelings of contentment may be temporary or illusory; they're all you've got. Snatch them up and enjoy them while they last.

32. Never underestimate the tremendous healing power of sitting down together from time to time to speak frankly and openly about the marital difficulties facing other couples you know.

33. The Department of Health currently recommends that men should drink no more than twenty-one units of alcohol per week, and women fourteen, a consumption ratio of three to two. This does not mean you can divide a bottle of wine according to these proportions. If you're married, it's half each—guidelines be damned.

34. A little paranoia is a good thing in marriage; complacency is the more dangerous enemy. You should never feel so secure in your partnership that you are unable to imagine the whole thing falling apart over a long weekend. I can't give you an exact figure for how many sleepless nights per year you should spend worrying that you're going to die alone and unhappy if you don't get your shit together spouse-wise, but it's somewhere between five and eight.

35. Try to speak at least once during the day, every day. If nothing else, it keeps vital channels of communication open and operating.

My wife has a habit of ringing me in the middle of the afternoon, wherever she is. Often there is some cryptic pretext for the call ("Measure our sofa and tell me how deep it is") but occasionally she checks in for no reason.

"Anything to report?" she says.

"I'm watching a YouTube compilation of dogs wearing shoes for the first time," I say.

"Sounds rewarding," she says.

"I mean the dogs are wearing the shoes for the first time. I've actually seen it a number of times already."

"I won't keep you, then," she says. "Take the mince out of the freezer."

It doesn't sound like much, but on such regular exchanges of inanities are rock-solid marriages built.

36. Most marriage counselors recommend that you say five positive things to your partner to counteract every negative thing you say. If five sounds like a lot to you—and it sounds like a lot to me—that ratio at least gives you an idea of the impact of a single negative comment. Dole them out as if they were unbelievably expensive.

37. On those occasions when you cannot bring yourself to say what you feel, at least try to act as though you feel what you say. If you're going to insist that everything's fine, then you should have the decency to behave as if everything is fine.

38. Every partnership is unique: don't feel the need to judge the success of yours in comparison to other relationships you see out there. For the most part, whatever you do to make it work between you is fine, even if no one else seems to handle things in quite the same way. You're even entitled to cherish your relationship's quirks and odd accommodations—just don't mention them to any psychologists you meet at dinner parties.

39. It's never too late to apologize. By which I mean, when it's obviously far too late for saying sorry to do any good at all, you still should.

40. Never bother me when I'm reading. For the sake of balance I asked my wife to contribute a Gross Marital Happiness tip of her own, and this

is what she said. My guess is that sooner or later she's going to regret not taking proper advantage of this opportunity.

41. It's okay to talk about your kids when you go out to a restaurant together. You're with the only other person who's actually interested in your kids. Seize the moment.

42. In marriage it's good to express your emotions freely, bar one: surprise. Unless you've just arrived at your own surprise birthday party, looking surprised can be dangerous. It means you've either forgotten something important, or you've misjudged a situation badly. Remember: if you don't look surprised, you aren't surprised.

9.

Bringing Home the Bacon

I have been married for nearly a year. I'm doing all the things that traditional husbands do, apart from providing. Having spent two years more or less unemployed, I do at least have a job, entering basic information about films into an enormous database. It's one of those odd occupations that existed before web 2.0 came along and the public was somehow persuaded to fill in the Internet themselves, for free.

But it doesn't pay much, my new job. And it doesn't really have a future, beyond the implicit promise that there will always be more data to enter the next day. My wife is working at the BBC, making programs and earning considerably more than me. I have decided that I am modern enough not to let this shame me, but I am not comfortable enough with the situation to imagine things can stay this way. My small financial contribution is vital, but it also isn't enough.

With my twenties behind me, I no longer have much in the way of prospects. For the previous two years I'd done little beyond sitting at the bar of the restaurant where my friend Pat worked, downing free espresso and doing the crossword.

Although I have a degree in English, the only actual skill I possess is basic page layout—the sort of cutting and pasting of copy that involves actual cutting and pasting, with a knife and glue—an occupation that basically disappeared on both sides of the Atlantic during the two years I spent sitting on my ass drinking coffee. Moving to London amounted to starting again from rung one.

In truth the peak of my career had occurred several years before, when I was parking cars outside a restaurant in Boston. It was possible to earn $300 in tips in a night, although $80 to $100 was more the norm. It was a high-adrenaline profession—we had no actual car park, so we worked in pairs to compete for spaces on the streets and in the allies. During my brief training the rules of parking were explained to me by a seasoned valet known as The Iceman. Rule one was "It's okay to hit the car in front." Rule two was "It's okay to hit the car behind." Rule three was "It's okay to steal pot from people's glove compartments."

I got mugged on my first shift, but I went straight back the next night. The hours meant I could hold down another job during the day, and it was as close as I'd ever come in my life to making ends meet. All the time I'd been working at the magazine in New York, I'd been gently tipping into financial ruin.

The months of idleness that followed were not initially difficult—I am naturally indolent; it's a gift—but both my wife and I had, I think, similar expectations of what a proper man should be, and I was not living up to them. She accepted that circumstances had prevented my working, but I could sense she found my lack of ambition irritating and disappointing, largely because I'd seen this disappointment in other women before. Back when I was still parking cars, my future as an embittered underachiever must have seemed set in stone.

I suppose I did have vague ambitions, or at least desired some sort of future for myself. I didn't know what it was, exactly, but I had a fair idea what it wasn't, which is why I would quit any job as soon as somebody tried to promote me. I wasn't actively bad at most of the paid work I undertook, but I was afraid of getting stuck on a rung some-where, and I preferred to keep moving. If you're willing to delude yourself, change can feel like progress.

I quit my job at the ice factory after three weeks, shortly after they moved me from block ice to bagged cubes. When they offered to make me assistant manager of the art shop where I worked, provided I was prepared to "work on my attitude," I worked hard to make sure my attitude got steadily worse. Then I quit.

A couple of years later, when I was temping in

the financial aid department of Northeastern University in Boston, my supervisor called me into his office. I thought it was probably about my timekeeping, or the tie I wasn't wearing.

"You've only been here three weeks," he said, "and you've revolutionized our filing system. What's your secret?"

"Alphabetical order," I said.

"I'm not sure why you'd want to be facetious at this point," he said. I rarely spoke at work, and sometimes had trouble controlling my tone.

"Seriously," I said. "I just put things back where they go." I hadn't meant to be facetious; it was clear to me, from all the times I'd tried to retrieve a file, that few of my predecessors had considered alphabetical order to be a guiding principle.

My tone notwithstanding, he said he was willing to consider me for a permanent staff position, with better money, paid vacations, and health insurance. So I quit.

Even the failing magazine in New York offered me a belated promotion when I told them I was planning to leave. But I already had a plane ticket to London and a big, blank future ahead of me, so I quit.

That's how I got to be thirty years old, newly married, and still at the foot of the ladder. The previous two years of doing nothing—of sacrificing money for love—had proved more than a little dispiriting. Being a loser, dependent on your girlfriend for a packet of fags, was, in the end, hard work.

My only plan is to put all that behind me, to stick at my new dead-end job and keep an eye out for a better one. I figure I don't need a career path anymore. Being married can be my career; I can be professionally uxorious. All I need is the money.

One August afternoon I get a call from someone who works at *GQ* magazine. The woman at the other end is, she explains, a friend of a friend of mine, but I don't really understand why she's calling me. I haven't applied for a job at *GQ*. It seems unlikely that my reputation for data entry precedes me.

"We have a regular section at the back of the magazine called 'Man Enough,' " she says. "It's a different topic every month."

"Uh-huh."

"And we'd like you to write one, if you want to; they're about seven hundred fifty words." I suppose I'd dreamed that something like this would happen to me one day, although I somehow figured I would have to be the one who dialed the number first. I can't figure out how such an offer could just drop into my lap. Then I think: Who cares how?

"Yeah," I say. "Great. What's the subject?"

"It'll be 'Man Enough to Live Off Your Girl-friend.' "

"Oh, right," I say.

Nobody enjoys being summarized. We each have a sense of self that is fluid, expanding, and resistant to definition. That's why it's so painful to read a potted biography of yourself, even when you've written it yourself. I am so much more than this tepid little précis, you think. Words can't contain me.

Now I was being presented with a seven-word summation which, for all I know, is how everyone described me when I was out of the room, or when distinguishing me from other Tims of their acquaintance: you know—the one who lives off his girlfriend.

I realize I have been silent for a long time.

"I could send over some copies of the magazine," says the woman on the phone, "so you get the general idea."

The general idea is clear from the three back issues I receive the next day: the monthly topic for the first-person "Man Enough" column was evidently selected by the editorial staff, who then went in search of a real-life man who fit the bill. I suppose they just asked round until someone of their acquaintance said, "Somebody who doesn't work? Who just sponges off his girlfriend and does nothing all day? Yeah, I know a dude like that."

I don't think being an actual writer is a prerequisite for the slot, which is just as well. In the course of my recently acquired day job I'd summarized the plots of four thousand films I'd never seen, but it doesn't amount to much of a cuttings file.

I don't say anything about my inexperience, nor do I mention that I am now both married and gainfully employed. I just say yes.

What I wrote did not do much to challenge the stigma that came with being a man who was not the chief earner in a relationship. Instead, if I recall correctly, I embraced that stigma and reveled in it.

It's not the sort of piece one could write today. In an economy that generally obliges both halves of a couple to work in order to survive, in an era where wage parity is, if not a reality, a commonly accepted goal, and where employment markets are increasingly fluid, we're a lot more at ease with the idea of a man who earns less than his partner, or earns nothing. In nearly a third of couples with children today, the mothers are considered breadwinners, in that they earn as much as or more than their partners.

Nor is it strange these days for the man in a partnership to be the one who works from home, or the one who works part-time, or not at all. Since 1993 the number of stay-at-home dads in the UK has doubled, while the number of women who stay home to look after children has dropped by about a third. Put that way, it sounds like a wholesale revolution, but it actually equates to about a million more mothers going out to work, and only a hundred thousand or so extra dads staying behind to take up the slack. Even so, by last year the stay-at-home dad was a sufficiently widespread phenomenon to earn it an honored place in the *Daily Mail*'s demonic social pantheon, courtesy of a self-excoriating article titled "I was so proud to be a stay-at-home dad. Now I fear it's harmed my daughter."

Even outside the *Daily Mail*'s peculiar world-view, the loss of self-esteem that comes from being a financially supported man lingers. I've felt it. I felt it for so long that I got used to it. I'd even begun to accept the possibility that it would always be that way, because I'd moved countries and altered the course of my life without much thought about how I was going to earn a living. My wife kept working, and I continued to be a drain on resources. A drain on resources who, frankly, should have been shouldering a larger share of the laundry.

It probably shouldn't be like this, because, by and large, men work too hard. It's one of the biggest regrets of dying people, particularly men: I wish I hadn't worked so hard. Men miss out on watching their children grow up, on holidays, on their marriages, on the weird private passions that consume them, all so they can work more, and harder.

If you are lucky, you might end up with a job you can't wait to start in the morning, work that brings you satisfaction, pleasure, and pride along with generous compensation for your time and effort. You won't need to strike a work-life balance, because you'll be too busy having a really nice work life.

But most men have to work at jobs they don't particularly enjoy in order to make money, doing stupid or humiliating things just because someone in charge told them to. If you don't believe happy-go-lucky freelance writers like me ever have this problem, I can only direct your attention to a thirteen-hundred-word feature about me dressing up as a bus conductor and traveling round central London trying to lure commuters onto a cattle truck. Or the day I spent at Santa school. Or the eight-hundred-word piece about bananas that I wrote on 9/11—while the world turned inside out, I spent the afternoon ringing up chefs and asking for banana recipes. I'd have to do a lot of humiliating things in the future for that one not to make my Top Ten Deathbed Regrets.

We hear a lot about the rise in the number of stay-at-home dads, and the increase in the number of households where women are the main—or sole—breadwinners, but these undoubted shifts don't necessarily paint an accurate picture of where we are right now. British fathers still work the longest hours in the EU—those with children under eleven work an average of forty-eight hours a week. Even in this fast-changing world, it would be fair to assume that over the course of their lives most men still strike a work-life balance that has too much work in it. As long as our self-esteem continues to be bound up in our capacity to earn, to achieve, and to provide, the bulk of the nation's husbands and fathers will continue to work a lot more than they want to, or perhaps even need to. As a result they will suffer from stress, from both the pressure of work and the need to juggle family commitments.

Surely as a father one has a greater obligation to provide time, attention, and unsolicited advice than disposable income. It's the same with being a husband—more breakups are caused by couples not spending enough time together than by an insufficiency of money. If wealth kept people happily married, rich people would never get divorced.

None of this is really my problem because I, for one, don't work too hard. I am both my own boss and my most troubling employee. My time is badly organized, and my highly variable work-load always stretches to fill the available time—back when I was writing an article a month, it took me a month to write an article. In all the

152

time we've been married my wife has never had to sit me down and tell me to take it easy.

However, having spent years trying not to let work define me because I didn't have any work, I now rather enjoy being able to claim occupational status, especially when family life encroaches on my employment (for this reason I always bring a little bit of work with me on holiday, just in case). I may not work too hard, but I work from home, so as far as I'm concerned I'm always at work.

"Somebody needs to go to Sainsbury's," says my wife, ringing my office from the kitchen on a weekday afternoon.

"This is my private work time," I say. "Imagine that I am in a meeting."

"It's difficult," she says, "because I can hear you playing a harmonica."

"It's a madhouse up here today," I say. "Seriously."

You will have heard about home workers succumbing to stress, or putting in fifteen more hours a week than their office-based counterparts. That ain't me. I do have stressful interludes, busy days, and hectic weeks. Very occasionally I take on too much work by accident, but even if I spent the next ten years pulling twelve-hour shifts in a salt mine, I still wouldn't be able to catch up with the average overworked male. When politicians talk about rewarding ordinary, hardworking people, I pay no attention, because I know they can't possibly be referring to me. I don't want the rewards they're offering in any case, which generally come in the form of small amounts of money taken from someone who needs it more.

Frankly, you couldn't pay me to work harder, because I can't put a price on my sloth. Just this morning, at a time when most people are arriving at their offices, I was falling asleep in the bath. I tipped my whole coffee into it when I conked out, which is why my arms are now a manly brown and give off the faint aroma of an Ecuadorian mountain cooperative. Trust me: you don't want to smell like money; you want to smell like coffee, like me.

My first magazine article appears on the back page of the November 1993 issue of *GQ* magazine. There is even a reference to it on the cover, alongside Sean Bean's face. It says, "RENT BOY—How to live off your girlfriend." I have mixed emotions. Making the cover of a magazine on your first go seems like an achievement to be proud of. At the same time, I don't think I should send a copy to my mother.

For years afterward I would receive the occasional call from a production assistant who, having found that *GQ* article in a cuttings file, tracked down my details in order to ask whether

I might be interested in going on the radio, or on daytime TV, to discuss the ins and outs of being a shiftless, unapologetic scumbag.

"The thing is," I would say, "I wrote that piece, like, seven years ago. My life isn't really like that anymore."

"I see," the voice at the other end would say, sounding terribly disappointed.

"I'm actually pretty busy these days," I'd say. "In fact, I've just started writing a column for the . . ."

"So it's all working out for you," says the voice. I'm clearly making someone's bad day at the office worse.

"Sorry," I say.

Despite my late start in journalism, things progressed slowly but steadily after that first *GQ* article. I became a regular contributor to the magazine and started writing for other publications. It was a long time, however, before I had the nerve to give up my day job to be nothing but a freelance writer. I suspected it was possible to earn more money if I could spend all day ringing people up and pitching them ideas, but I also knew myself better than that.

Also, my wife kept mentioning that she was pregnant.

10.

A Very Short Chapter About Sex

I would dearly love to assume that no one wants to read about my sex life, largely because I don't really want to write about it. Even a sexually confident, well-adjusted man might wish to draw a veil over this facet of his business, and I am neither of those things. And also, my wife forbade me to write about it, thank Christ.

But you can't write a book about being a husband and just skip sex, according to certain publishers I know. Even if sex is no longer marriage's unique selling point, it remains an important component of any union, and in that context it deserves at least cursory treatment in a brief chapter all its own. You may, if you wish, infer that the following highly informative sexual bullet points have been gleaned from decades of personal experience, but officially, I learned all this from watching television.

- There is an old and unattractive joke which holds that marriage isn't about having sex with the same person for the rest of your life, but about *not* having sex with the same person for the rest of your life. There is a depressing truth to this. While the actual amount of sex undertaken will vary from couple to couple, there is no getting round the fact that marriage is in part an epic exercise in sexual rejection. Being a good husband means hearing the word "no" (variants include "stop it," "fuck off," "leave me alone") countless times over many years without going hot in the face with hurt and self-loathing, or at least not appearing to. It means gallantly turning down halfhearted offers of perfunctory, mechanical sex from someone too tired to contemplate anything else, and then finding a way, five minutes later, to say that you've changed your mind.

• Not having very much sex is not just normal, it's the norm. According to the National Survey of Sexual Attitudes and Lifestyles (Natsal), people between the ages of sixteen and forty-four have sex, on average, less than once a week. The rate has been falling steadily, even among cohabiting couples (a mean of four times a month, down from five a decade ago) for some time, with experts variously seeking to blame either the recession, higher stress levels, or the increasing use of smartphones and tablets in the bedroom. There is one upside: you don't have to have sex very often in order to be having more than most people.

• Believe it or not, if you're married you're almost certainly having more sex than you would be if you were single. If you were single, chances are you'd be having none.

• If wanting more sex than you're getting is a depressingly common state of affairs, it is quite possibly preferable to having more sex than you want. There are points during a marriage where you may briefly experience the latter. Let's imagine for the sake of argument that your wife's desire for a second child has not been answered with the immediacy—indeed the surprise—that attended the conception of the first—and you find yourself obliged to investi-gate the mechanics of fertility with an eye toward improving your odds. Under these trying circumstances you will, as the preferred sperm supplier, find yourself more or less on call, required to perform often and at short notice, with little in the way of preliminary chat, beyond an admonition to get the job done before *Coronation Street* starts. You will learn what it's like, perhaps for the first and only time in your life, to have so much sex at your disposal that it becomes an inconvenience. You should probably find someone to complain about it to, in case you never get the chance again.

• No matter how much of a traditional British male you consider yourself to be, you must eventually learn to have sex while sober. If you don't, twenty years of marital bliss will kill you.

• The basic strategies for maintaining a healthy sex life are not, in themselves, sexy. It has a lot more to do with emptying the dishwasher without being asked than you think. I'm sorry about this.

• If you can't do it with the cat watching, you're probably not as interested as you think you are.

• Sex, for the most part, happens between couples who go to bed at the same time. It's fine to stay up later than your partner, as long as you bear in mind that you are effectively choosing between sex and *Newsnight*. Waking up your partner for sex is famously not a good idea, although I've always imagined I would be totally accommodating about it if it ever happened to me.

• Strive to have sex regularly, even if you don't feel like it. This is not my personal tip—lots of relationship experts advocate it—although I'm pretty sure the words "even if you don't feel like it" have escaped my lips before. The trick is to forget all about passion, spontaneity, and experimentation. True carnal open-mindedness extends to embracing the idea that run-of-the-mill sex is still worth having.

• Don't just wait for the right moment to have sex. Schedule the right moment. Be punctual.

• Scheduled sex is no guarantee of sex, mind. When the appointed hour rolls round you may find your best-laid plans unceremoniously vetoed, or at least undermined. If your partner greets your prebooked advances with the words "Is it the first Friday of the month already?" you may safely assume she's attempting to sabotage the mood.

• According to some other experts the secret of long-term sexual attraction is a carefully maintained air of mystery: discretion regarding nudity, the banishment of domestic drudgery from the bedroom, and some boundaries regarding one another's bodily functions and ablutions. I'm not saying I agree or disagree. I'm just saying: good luck with that.

• Young men: your talent for being able

to get sex over and done with really quickly is probably not much prized at the moment, but it will come in handy down the road, so don't forget how. It may be hard to believe at your age, but one day you'll reach a stage in your relationship where "Honestly—you'll hardly know I was here" becomes a surprisingly successful chat-up line, especially if your spouse knows you can deliver on the promise.

11.

The Pros and Cons
of Procreation

Being a father is a fairly standard adjunct to being a husband. It's not mandatory, of course, but it's considered churlish to refuse.

There are many different ways for a couple to broach the delicate conversation about starting a family, the most traditional of which, in my experience, begins with the woman saying, "I don't believe this—I'm fucking pregnant."

That only happened the first time, to be fair. In later years my wife would simply emerge from the loo and throw the positive pregnancy test at me. As magical as each of these moments were, it is my suggestion that you and your partner give serious consideration to the idea of having children intentionally, with an eye on a fixed total, not least because they cost £67,000 each just to feed and clothe. The ideal number is a very personal choice. I have three, so I know that for me, three is too many.

When you first discover you're going to be a father, you will be giddy, but also filled with a sense that something terrifying and life-changing is about to happen to you. The present becomes tinged with an ominous hue, like the glow of a warehouse fire on the horizon. After a few weeks you will be struck by the sudden realization that the terrifying thing isn't going to happen to you at all. It's going to happen to someone else, and you are going to watch. It's still going to be terrifying, but you should not say that out loud. In fact, the complete etiquette for male behavior in the first and second trimester can be boiled down to a list of things you shouldn't say to a pregnant woman. They include, but are by no means limited to, the following:

"I know what you mean—my back is killing me."

"I think I'm losing weight. Do I look thin to you?"

"Thanks for driving. I'm absolutely hammered."

"Let's face it—it's not an illness, is it?"

"A hundred quid for a car seat? Are they high?"

Above all else the partners of pregnant women are expected to be supportive, "supportive" being one of those terms that has caused a whole generation of men to nod while furrowing their brows slightly, in a feeble attempt to impersonate comprehension. Once upon a time "supportive" could be understood to refer to financial and/or material support, and when someone spoke of your need to be supportive, they were basically hinting that now would be a really bad time for you to get fired.

Allow me, with all the benefit of my experience, to translate the woolly imperative "Be supportive" into a more man-friendly command: in the context of pregnancy, it means "Suck it up." Repress any instinct to express needs or to share counter-productive emotions, for the duration.

You don't want to spend a Saturday shopping for a crib fully six months in advance of having anything to put in it? Suck it up.

Don't feel like going along to prenatal class? Suck it up. I was the only man who turned up to my first one, and I was made to lie on a mat and exercise my vagina for half an hour. All the women there later told my wife that I was very brave and caring, which made me feel a bit bad about running off during the first tea break.

Don't fancy spending another night arguing with someone who suddenly thinks Howard is a good name for boy? Suck it up. But don't give in on Howard.

Suck up the anger, the tears, and the tiredness. Not yours—hers. You should have sucked up yours, like, yesterday.

You will probably still feel that you are not doing anything much, beyond exhibiting a certain resentful forbearance. You may never again in your life feel quite this useless. I suggest you find a displacement activity that gives you a sense of being proactively preparatory, like a father-in-waiting should be. Select something important you lack, and fix it. Take butchery lessons, or a first aid course. The choice is yours. Me, I learned to drive.

Actually I already knew how to drive, but as a UK resident, my American license had ceased to be valid. By the time my wife became pregnant with our first child, I hadn't driven a car for three years. The longer I went on not driving, the easier it became. My wife drove everywhere while I looked out the window, or dozed while drooling onto my seat belt. Secretly, I loved not driving.

But even I could not imagine strapping my first child into his car seat in the hospital car park, and then slipping into the passenger seat while my postpartum wife eased herself behind the wheel and checked her mirrors. I don't actually think it would have been allowed, but I wasn't stupid enough to ask anyone. I just went out and signed up for a load of driving lessons.

I can't say I enjoyed it much. One of the things that got me through driving lessons the first time round was the thought that once I'd passed, I would not have to repeat the ordeal under any circumstances. Never again would I have to spend four hours a week pretending to be in accord with the personal prejudices of a right-wing lunatic with a brake of his own. Never again would I have my parallel parking technique criticized by someone I have come to hate. Never again would I need to grip the wheel in the ten-and-two position. If you'd told me at seventeen that fourteen years later I'd be going through the whole terrible business again, but in a foreign country, on the wrong side of the road, and with an even fatter and more objectionable man in the passenger seat, I think I would have lost the strength to carry on. Certainly there were times during my second period of indoctrination that I thought about giving up. But I told myself, "This is the only thing you could think of doing to make it seem as if you were training up for parenthood. If you fail at this, you fail at everything."

I persevered, and passed my test the first time. I kept the results to show my heavily pregnant wife that whatever she thought of my driving, the Driver and Vehicle Licensing Agency thought different. And none of my children would ever have to meet the me that didn't drive.

My wife's waters break one night in the middle of *EastEnders*. There follows some debate about whether we should watch the end before going to the maternity ward. This is partly an attempt by two very nervous people to appear calm and wise before the fact: there's no hurry; we're already packed; why not? But it's also a last-minute scrabble for purchase before we tumble over the lip of the unknown. Our lives are, by all accounts, about to be turned upside down. For all we know we may never have the luxury of caring about *EastEnders* again. And Peggy Mitchell's just moved back to the Vic and has no idea that Sharon and Grant are quits on account of Sharon's affair with Phil no longer being a secret. Life in the square is absolutely mental at the moment.

As soon as the credits roll we go downstairs and get in the car. My wife insists on taking a long detour to the nearest McDonald's drive-thru. We haven't had supper and she doesn't know when she'll eat next. It will be many hours before this seems like a stupid idea.

At the hospital we check in and my wife is examined. Everything appears to be normal, but labor proper is apparently some way off. We wait and wait. At some point a nurse suggests that I go home and get some sleep. This is put to me as the most practical and sensible thing to do in the circumstances. To me, it sounds insane, but I'm offered no other options and I have a strong desire to be counted among the rational. Eventually, I go. I'm convinced I won't be able to sleep, but I surprise myself.

It's still dark when the phone I have placed halfway up the stairs to our attic bedroom—as far as its cord will reach—starts ringing. I have forgotten about this arrangement and trip over it on my way down. I end up on all fours on the landing feeling around for the loose receiver.

"Is that Mr. Dowling?" says a voice, in response to the crash and muffled swearing I have substituted for "hello."

"Yes," I say.

"Things are progressing nicely here," she says, "so this would probably be a good time to maybe start thinking about making your way in." I have not lived in England so long that I can instantly grasp the meaning of a sentence like this at six a.m. There is a brief silence while I parse.

"So you're saying I should come now."

"That might be an idea," she says.

My wife is not the same person I left behind the night before. Then she was apprehensive but pragmatic, largely worried that she might be lonely or bored. In the intervening hours she has been transformed by pain into a wild thing. Between contractions she tells me how she spent the night stalking the corridors, a V-shaped pillow over one shoulder, in search of a dark, quiet corner, like an animal looking for a place to die. At one point, she says, she shut herself in a supply cupboard for half an hour. The cheeseburger she ingested—however temporarily—has long since been relegated to the very least of her present regrets; top of the list is getting pregnant, followed by meeting me.

"Where have you been?" she says, eyes darting one way and another. She's outside the ward, leaning against a wall as another contraction begins.

"I'm sorry," I say. "They only rang me twenty minutes ago."

"Don't touch me," she says. "Just take this stupid pillow." I lift it gently off her back and shoulder it like a Samaritan, with all the depthless inadequacy the gesture implies.

In retrospect it is a mercy that I had no experience of childbirth, that there were no weekly TV programs detailing the quotidian heroics of midwives, the general uncomprehending idiocy of fathers-to-be or the sheer number of things that can go wrong during a routine delivery. I'm glad I had no idea that an epidural was not just tricky to administer but rather difficult to procure, like an item on a specials menu the waiter keeps trying to talk you out of.

I'm glad I had no notion then, as I do now, that being an effective liaison between a woman in labor and the maternity ward staff requires rather more insistence than mediation, or that "I'm sure someone will be back in a minute" is not a helpful thing to say. I feel fortunate that I only learned about the true role of the father in childbirth—to be perpetually in the way, until someone finally suggests you go down the hall and make everyone some tea—on the job, and knew nothing of the impotent, hand-wringing anguish beforehand.

The midwife is still desperate to get me involved. As labor enters its final stage she hands me a damp cloth.

"You dab Mum's forehead with that," she says. "It will help keep her cool and calm."

"Got it," I say.

I go up to the other end of the bed, round the back of the heart monitor. I wait until another contraction begins, and then I lean forward and tentatively blot my wife's hairline with one corner of the cloth.

"Get that fucking thing away from my face," she says.

"Okay," I say.

I'm pleased that on that day I'd never before heard the term "placenta previa," and that the whole event occurred before the age of the smartphone, when I could have found out what it meant in an instant. I was in the lucky position of being able to assume that nothing out of the ordinary was occurring, and that there was always that much blood left over at the end. I'm pleased that the nature of the complication was never fully explained to me, so that by the time I understood what had almost happened, the danger had already passed.

Thanks to my ignorance I could, in all honesty, simply savor the profound emotional head butt of childbirth, directing all my attention to my exhausted, parchment-pale wife and the little purple creature in the plexiglass box. I could just stand there and cry, not out of fear, but with the simple relief of a man who has been allowed to take a short break from being overwhelmed.

It is well into the afternoon when the whole business is finished. While my wife's being topped up with blood products, I am dispatched home again to spread the news: it's a boy.

When I return to the hospital a few hours later I find my wife sitting cross-legged in the middle of her bed, eating an apple and staring down at the sleeping infant lying on the mattress in front of her.

I hang back for a few seconds without making my presence known. It is a scene that remains burned into my memory, indelible as a photograph, and the first instance of my feeling that peculiar sense of left-outness that comes with being a father. My wife is staring down at our son with the boundless but unremarkable fascination one reserves for parts of oneself long unseen: a broken foot finally freed after months in a cast. There was nothing I had witnessed about pregnancy or childbirth that made me feel I was somehow missing out—what I saw, you can keep—but this, I see in a glimpse, is the beginning of an intimacy I will never have with anyone or anything. Perhaps, as a man, I'm even a little frightened by it. It's not remotely mystical, but undeniably physical and matter-of-fact. I won't say visceral; I stopped using the word "visceral" for a long time after that day.

In the first weeks of fatherhood my collective responsibilities fail to coalesce into anything I could describe as a role. It is, for the most part, donkey work: I clean, I run errands, I change the odd nappy.

When it comes to parenting I'm basically an understudy, ready to step in and distract the baby for short periods so my wife can use the phone. The child requires more or less the same things from his mother as his father; it's just that he prefers all of them to come from his mother: feeding, dressing, reading, eye contact.

As he develops the rudiments of coordination, the boy starts to see me largely as an object for experimental violence. He sticks his fingers in my eyes and tries to push small objects up my nose. He sinks his fingernails into my throat while I am carrying him up the stairs. I pretend not to mind. If it can be considered in any way useful, I am happy to lie on the floor alongside an infant whose afternoon schedule is entirely taken up with trying to pull my lips off.

With no seeming knack for child care, I begin to take pride in the sheer stamina required to do it badly. I revel in the stoic, manly patience required to feed a mouth that is dodging the spoon for sport, or to secure a nappy round flailing legs. One day, I think, you'll be all grown up and changing my nappy. And oh, how I will kick. During the difficult times I picture myself as a tough but avuncular drill sergeant, the sort who leans close to your ear and says, "I'm not here to be liked, son."

But I *am* here to be liked. My life's mission is to trick people into liking me. If I can't make my own baby like me, what's the point?

His first word is "daddy," by which he means "mummy." His first complete sentence, coined for my benefit, is "Go away."

We rub along better when we're outside together, where preferring his mother is not an immediate option. I enjoy driving around with him strapped in behind me. Here he serves a valuable purpose: if he's in the car, then technically I'm not talking to myself.

By the end of the first year, I've learned a lot. I've learned how to prepare four bottles of formula in assembly-line fashion. I've learned to change a nappy in under a minute. I've learned to make a one-year-old laugh by pretending to cause myself harm. I've learned that in the event of a supermarket meltdown, the last thing you want to do is remove a wailing child from the trolley seat. You'll never get him back in.

Somewhere toward the end of this period I

quit my day job. I figure now is the perfect moment to become a full-time freelance writer, as oxymoronic as that job title turns out to be. It also means I can be around to wage my campaign to trick a baby into liking me. What I do not provide in money, I will make up for in sheer, unadulter-ated presence.

In the most technical sense, I become a stay-at-home dad, although I think of myself more as a layabout-with-child. I'm not sure people even spoke of stay-at-home dads back then—"house-husband" was the more common term for the less common thing.

By quitting my day job I come to fulfill the letter, if not the spirit, of the distinction. My wife is not ashamed of my new at-home status, although she is at pains to point out to people that there's a big difference between a househusband and a shut-in. During business hours I'm more like a helpful upstairs neighbor whose job happens to be staring out the window all day.

I look like a stay-at-home dad, though, especially if you see me at the zoo with two toddlers at three p.m. on a Wednesday, when it happens that I have nothing better to do. If it's a Saturday, I look like a divorced dad. If it's the supermarket and it's Saturday, I just look incompetent.

The vast of bulk of my parenting is done as half of a tag team—lurching from crisis to crisis, making up policy on the fly, and presenting a united front despite marked differences in approach. My wife and I share the more tedious aspects of infant-rearing equally, at least in the sense that neither of us ever does anything without having a crack at getting the other to do it first.

"He's crying again," says my wife, gently punching me awake.

"Oh God—why are my eyes so dry? I must have been sleeping with them open."

"Deal with him," says my wife.

"But I went half an hour ago," I say.

"He's your child, and he's crying," she says. "It's not about whose turn it is."

"You're saying that," I say, "because it's your turn."

"Go."

"I think he's stopped now," I say.

"He hasn't."

"So what, shall I bring him back here for you?"

"No."

It's not ideal, but it's the system. Coparenting, I think they call it.

12.

Alpha Male, Omega Man

A few years ago I wrote a novel. For our purposes there are only four things you need to know about this book:

1. It failed to set the world alight, and then, eight months later, it failed to set the world alight again, in paperback.

2. Despite this double failure, it's actually not bad at all.

3. It is now available on Kindle.

4. It contains a brief scene in which the main character, a freelance journalist, is rung up by a newspaper commissioning editor, and asked the following question:

"Would you describe yourself as an alpha male?"

Not understanding the purpose of the question, the writer refuses to give a straight answer. The commissioning editor goes on to say that a recent study has suggested that alpha males are evolutionarily unsuited to our modern, feminized society, that the aggression and dominant posturing that once gave them an advantage is now counterproductive. He wishes to commission fifteen hundred words about the lesser male types—the beta males, the gammas, the deltas—in a particularly base form of journalism known as an alphabet piece.

"So what we want from you," he says, "is the whole Greek alphabet, all the males from alpha to omega, but funny."

I made up this little scene, fiction-style, not to illustrate some point about the quiet rise—or not—of nonalpha men, but simply to furnish my main character with the worst journalistic assignment imaginable. An alphabet piece is a horrible prospect on its own—it's a hackneyed, spent format, with the intolerable burden of having to come up with twenty-six separate gags, and the inevitable need to fudge the entries for Q and X. For all the work required, they're never as funny as they should be. I ought to know—I've written a fair few in my time. What, I thought, could possibly inspire more dread in a weary freelance hack than another pointless alphabet piece? Then I thought: What if you had to use Greek letters instead?

In the novel the main character tries, and fails, to turn the assignment down. He displays a marked lack of enthusiasm for the idea, and insists its successful execution lies beyond his limited capabilities. He demurs from several angles, to no avail.

"You're definitely not an alpha male, by the way," says the editor. "I'd put you somewhere around tau."

178

"I don't even know where that comes," says the writer.

Writing this scene was, as I recall, a pleasantly cruel morning's work. In the end, however, the joke was on me: a few days later I realized the narrative would be best served by reproducing the fictional article in full, so I had to sit down and write the whole fucking thing myself. It took me a week and a half, and I only managed twelve hundred words. I was as glad to have it behind me as any assignment I have ever accepted.

Six years later I am sitting in my office minding my own business when my phone rings. The person on the other end is a researcher from the radio program *Woman's Hour*. She says she wants to speak to me about alpha males.

Alpha males are on the wane, she tells me. A recent magazine article has claimed that their hypercompetitive, domineering personalities put them at a distinct disadvantage in our modern, feminized society. According to somebody somewhere, beta males are taking over the world. A sense of déjà vu begins to steal over me as she speaks.

"So," she says finally. "Would you describe yourself as an alpha male or a beta male?"

"I think I come somewhere around tau," I say. There is a pause.

"I don't know the Greek alphabet that well," she says.

There follows a brief discussion in which I characterize myself as a meek and inconsequential man. It is a sort of pre-interview, at the end of which I am invited to appear on *Woman's Hour*. I display a calculated lack of enthusiasm for the idea and suggest that it may lie beyond my limited broadcast capabilities. There is something about my low self-esteem that delights her.

That was the first time I ever felt the need to sit down and consider the whole concept of the alpha male in human society, and my first thought was: It's basically bollocks, isn't it? An alpha male is something you find in charge of a wolf pack. As a sociological term it doesn't mean much when applied to a species that shops at Uniqlo.

It turns out I was wrong: the term doesn't apply to wolves either. In the wild a typical wolf pack is dominated by what used to be known as an alpha male and an alpha female—an alpha couple—but biologists don't call them that anymore, because their elevated status within the pack is not due to size, aggression, or a keen sense of competition. It's because all the other wolves in the pack are their pups. A wolf pack is a family, and the alpha male is the daddy.

Chimps also produce alpha males, as do many primate groupings. But then bonobos, from the same genus as chimps, live in a society where females are dominant. In any case, the alpha male isn't a type—it's an office, and in a strictly linear dominance hierarchy, there's just one. Whether an alpha male's status is by dint of size, strength, age, aggression, or the assiduous grooming of others (much of the work of being an alpha chimp is tiresomely political), it's not really analogous to anything in human society. If chimps could get ahead by lying on their CVs, they would probably do it our way.

When we speak, perennially, of alphas males feeling out of place in a feminized society, what we're really talking about is the failure of men generally to adapt to a job market that increasingly prizes so-called soft skills—teamwork, dealing with the public, processing feedback—as well as women have. And it's arguably the stereotypical beta male—a salaried worker who's guaranteed a job as long as he does what's expected of him— who is really losing out. But the old corporate structures were never an unconscious replication of natural dominance hierarchies; we just made them up, and now they're being supplanted by something else.

Most of us know it's nonsense to divide the human male population into alphas and betas, but the concept is strangely embedded in popular culture. As society adjusts its priorities over time, our idea of what constitutes an alpha male has to be tweaked, lest the term become a mere synonym for "arsehole." A trawl through men's magazines and the sort of websites that feature pop-up ads for muscle supplements will turn up such revisionist alpha-male traits as "the ability to laugh at himself," "being a good listener," "apologizing for being wrong," "developing new skills," and "helping others." None of these would put you in mind of an alpha male like, say, Pol Pot, but so persistent is the notion of a top dog that we'd rather shoehorn some belated sensitivity into the definition than give up on it.

Perhaps our misplaced fondness for this construct is harmless, or no worse than attributing certain quirks of personality to a specific star sign. To bundle up a few traits—"competitive and loud," or "tall and promiscuous"—and give them a label may be nothing more than a convenient conversational shorthand. But the division of the male population into alphas and betas is part of the whole idea of masculinity as a zero-sum game, a competition where nice guys finish last. It reinforces a belief in a preordained system that allows your male boss to run a department and be a terrible cock at the same time. He's an alpha male. That's just the way the world works.

Above all this system comes packaged with an evolutionary imperative: women prefer alpha males, so either be one, or learn to fake it. This is the mantra of an unattractive subset of masculinity known as pickup artists (PUAs), who are always on the lookout for a pseudoscientific justification for a system they think gives them an advantage in "reproductive success," i.e., helps them have sex with damaged people they meet in bars. It's worth pointing out that genuine reproductive success—the creation of healthy progeny with three good A-levels—tends to occur only after you've stopped trying to pick up damaged people in bars.

Still, if women prefer alpha males, you as a man should definitely avoid giving out signals that you are anything else. Even at my age, I still feel a pang of shameful unmanliness whenever I am obliged to use one of those fake pound coins to liberate a shopping trolley from the stack. Our whole warped idea about what masculinity comprises hangs on such stupidities. Not all that long ago David Cameron accused Ed Miliband of being insufficiently "assertive and butch" because he occasionally got Ed Balls a coffee. Over the years innumerable other traits have been cited, seriously or jovially, as evidence of nonalpha status. They include:

> being a vegetarian
> not being able to drive
> eating quiche
> wearing glasses
> displaying a chronic reluctance to commit
>   assault
> allowing a woman to buy you dinner

taking the bus
sitting down to pee
knowing the names of flowers
owning an apron
working in the public sector

As a relaxed, confident, twenty-first-century male, you would probably allow yourself a few nonalpha behaviors without worry; personally, I would happily cop to five of the above. But I probably wouldn't dare to indulge all of them. To the extent that we are driven by the need to get and keep female companionship, we are risk averse, and the alpha-male myth still holds sway.

Of course, the world doesn't really work this way at all, as is reinforced every time I discover—to my unending surprise—that a man who sports an elaborately waxed mustache also has a girlfriend. As silly as the concept of the human alpha male is, it exerts a certain tyranny over our thinking. We need to free ourselves from its shackles.

The alpha-male myth is a by-product of evolutionary psychology—the theory that holds that while natural selection has shaped our thinking and behavior over millennia, our brains haven't evolved significantly since the Stone Age. We are effectively still cavemen, unsuited to the demands of modern society, slaves to our biology.

This premise, while not entirely suspect, is often questioned by evolutionary biologists. It may be plausible to suggest our brains haven't changed that much, but we have very little evidence to show how our ancestors of ten thousand years ago thought or behaved, and none to support the belief that humans ever lived in groups with the sort of hierarchical dominance one sees in modern chimpanzees. Our closest common ancestor lived six million years ago; we've both evolved a lot since then, in decidedly different directions.

Such evidence as we have seems to suggest that early humans banded together in egalitarian groups where efforts to dominate were punished. The idea that our human brains are an inheritance from forebears who lived in tribes with an alpha male at the top of the pecking order is pretty well fraudulent. Stop worrying about whether or not you're an alpha male. There is no such thing.

The morning after the phone conversation with the researcher I find myself in the *Woman's Hour* green room, drinking coffee, perspiring heavily and chatting to a man from Royal Mail who is publicizing a new commemorative stamp featuring Quaker campaigner Joan Mary Fry.

"So," he says, "what are you here to talk about?"

"Not being an alpha male," I say.

"Oh," he says. "I guess I'm not an alpha male either." I shrug. It seems unlikely, I think, with your diffident manner and your framed stamps. I have to remind myself that I've already decided there's no such thing as an alpha male.

When my time arrives I am conducted into the softly lit confines of the studio and seated behind a microphone, next to another male journalist, whom I imagine is there to offer an opinion that runs counter to mine. I try to remember what my opinion is. The presenter, Jenni Murray, addresses him first. As he speaks I desperately attempt to organize my revised thinking on the alpha-male myth and the need to resist its simplistic tyranny into a coherent philosophy, one that begins with a sentence that I can say right now. Finally Jenni Murray turns to me and asks where I would rank myself on the alpha/beta-male spectrum.

"Somewhere around lambda," I say.

13.

Coming to Grief

Three weeks after my mother-in-law's funeral, the phone rings. People are still calling every day to see how my wife is coping. It has been a long and terrible year of ambulances in the middle of the night, of hospitals, of bad news and worse news, of repeated, frightening dress rehearsals for mourning, brief reprieves, and finally, the grim business of day-to-day existence in grief's long shadow. Through all this I am repeatedly sur-prised by how little I have to offer. I had always imagined reserves of strength and maturity that I could dredge up for genuine emergencies. They're not there.

My wife is more than bereaved; she is post-traumatic. We have life-changing decisions to make—about the house, about the future—that we both seem incapable of thinking clearly about. The demands of a two-year-old are a welcome distraction, but child care takes everything out of us. Without quite saying so, we've more or less agreed to wait out this part of our lives, until such time as the knack for looking forward to things returns.

My wife has stopped talking on the phone; she

is holding it out to me. "It's your sister," she says.

There is a faint hiss with a rackety pulse to it on the line, which I first mistake for the hollow whoosh of long distance. Only when I press my ear closer to the receiver do I realize that it's the breathing of someone who has been—who still is—crying.

"Mom's sick," says my sister.

Our mother, she tells me, has been diagnosed with pancreatic cancer. I listen, waiting for the good news at the end, but there is no good news. Although she's scheduled for surgery, the long-term treatment she's been offered is largely palliative. She's been given between a year and eighteen months to live.

I ring my mother, who is being unbearably upbeat for my sake. Or maybe she really is upbeat; I can't tell. The conversation is unprecedented.

A couple of weeks later I learn that despite the bad news my family is pressing ahead with a trip to the US Senior Olympics in Arizona, where my father has qualified to compete. I make plans to join them; it's about the soonest I can get away anyway. It's not a good time to leave my wife, bereaved and in charge of a small child and, as she keeps mentioning, pregnant again. It's not a good time for anything.

I have to check that old passport—the index to my life—to remember how I actually spent that year. Apart from the trip to Arizona at the end of May, when I flew out to LA and drove to Tucson with my brother, it's clear that I visited home for two weeks in July and—that's it. My mother also came to London once some time before the middle one was born in January.

On all these occasions she seemed impossibly well to me. This impression probably contributed to my decision not to make any decisions. My brother left California to move closer to home, but packing up was not an option for me. I had a wife and two small children. A decade before, when I was twenty-seven, it didn't seem to matter where on the planet I chose to pitch my tent. I wasn't abandoning anyone, or giving anything up. I was just getting on with it. I didn't think about any eventualities that might make having two families—each with its own, competing priorities—on two continents awkward.

Just a year after the trip to Arizona, I am called back to Connecticut. My mother has taken a turn for the worse, and is at home recovering from a second operation. Only she's not really recovering. Come now, everyone is saying. I know what it means.

I fly over immediately, feeling like the Angel of Death. I imagine my mother taking one look at me and thinking, If he's here, I must really be in trouble.

This moment, in fact, happens twice. The

second morning after my arrival I am unable to wake my mother, and we have to ring an ambulance. She's in hypoglycemic shock—an injection brings her round immediately—but when I see her in hospital later on that day she has no memory of my previous arrival. I show her the pictures of the baby—already five months old—all over again.

In the drifting days that follow, a halting routine develops: visiting times divided into overlapping chunks, arranged rendezvous outside the hospital to pass all-day parking permits through car windows, swapping crossword clues in the long hours when my mother is asleep. When she's awake she's chatty and perfectly lucid, but seems only dimly aware of the passage of time. Every day might be the same day. And why not? Everything looks the same, and nobody's going anywhere.

Off the schedule there are appointments with nuns about church services, and grim trips to view available cemetery plots. In between, I work, getting up before dawn to file to British deadlines. Everything is last-minute and rushed, and yet this period has in my memory a languorous, dreamlike quality, as if it went on for months.

The parish priest drops in on his round of hospital visits, and offers to perform the last rites while he's at hand. It seems an awkward proposition to put to my mother: "We didn't call in a priest, honestly; he just happened to be in the area."

Fortunately, she is asleep. Under the circumstances none of us can offer any objection, although that's before we realize our participation will be required. I'd always assumed that everybody else left the room when extreme unction was administered, like when you have an X-ray done.

In spite of our reluctance the priest soon has us all joining hands around the bed with him. He begins with some informal opening remarks. Although I'm trying not to, I eventually catch my sister's eye, and I know we are both thinking the same thing: come on, Father—let's get it done.

Finally the priest starts intoning some actual prayer words. This is the moment my mother chooses to wake up—while her children are staring down at her, heads lowered, hand in hand, with a priest up the far end. I have a strong desire to pretend we're doing something else—playing a fun parlor game, or rehearsing a scene from *Godspell*—but alas, my mother has never been stupid.

"Thank you for the last rites, Father," she says.

I tell my wife the story when I call her later, although I don't think she finds it as morbidly amusing as I'm trying to make it sound. I guess you had to be there, I say. Then I take her through the latest round of difficulties. My mother isn't dying fast enough, as far as the hospital is concerned—either their admissions policy or my mother's insurance won't cover an open-ended leave-taking in an expensive hospital room. They're talking about putting her in a hospice two hours' drive from home, I say, possibly in a matter of days.

There is a silence on the other end of the line. My wife faced a similar dilemma when her mother refused to expire in accordance with the NHS's timetable. I imagine she's thinking about that.

"They're being very nice about it," I say. "But still."

"I need you to come back," my wife says.

It's one of those occasions when a correct response does not immediately present itself. She's right in one sense—she's on her own with two tiny children—but I am not in a position to get on a plane. I'm not even in a position to predict when I might be in a position to get on a plane. There is no right thing to do, just events, decisions, and their attendant consequences. If there is a delicate way to summarize the complex tangle of priorities I'm facing, I can't think of it.

"It's not like I'm on vacation here," I say. I have just been for a swim, though, which suddenly feels a bit disloyal.

"I know," my wife says. "I just need to be able to say it."

It was not, in the end, nearly as drawn out as I remember. My mother died on June 9, just four days after my birthday, when I modeled her present—a dark blue suit I would wear to her funeral—for her in her hospital room.

It's too late to ring home that night, so I call the next day.

"I'm sorry," my wife says. I look out the window; it's bright, almost cloudless—a reminder that the worst things happen on the nicest of summer days. Somewhere nearby, a lawn is being professionally cut. It's a Wednesday. You have to take tragedy as it comes—as part of the weft of the world's business—or not at all.

I don't remember much of the rest of our conversation. When I think about it now I usually recall another morning, a little over a year before—the morning my mother-in-law died. I was casting about for some way to offer comfort to my shell-shocked wife, and getting nowhere. After a long silence, she spoke up from the depths of her grief.

"You might as well go and get the car inspected," she said.

"Really?"

"Go on. We'll never get another appointment."

Sometimes, as a husband, you can offer no better help than to do as you are asked.

To my unending surprise, my passport shows I landed at Heathrow on the morning of June 19, my mother's funeral already behind me, less than three weeks after I'd left. Like the June nine years before, when I turned up with my bags having quit my job in New York, I arrive with a nagging sense that I am running away from something. This time, at least, that feeling is accompanied by the hope of coming home.

14.

Staying Together— for Better and Worse

You may have recited traditional marriage vows, or slightly reformed ones with the most blatantly sexist language removed. You may have written your own from scratch or, like me, you might have done little more than state your full name and admit no lawful impediment. In any case there will probably come a point in your marriage when you'll wish you'd made your requirements a bit clearer and your demands a bit more specific.

People often speak of unconditional love—the kind your dog has for you—as the very height of emotional experience, but marriage is meant to be the biggest relationship of your life, and it has nothing to do with unconditional love. "For better, for worse" isn't something you feel; it's something you promise. Marital love is, in fact, bounded on all sides by conditions: pull your weight, understand me, be faithful, bear in mind that you said you liked cats, tolerate my character flaws, agree with me about the state of this carpet, school our children in accordance with my principles, allow me to keep mustard in the fridge once it's been opened. Often these conditions are unspoken, but it doesn't mean they aren't there.

Unconditional love is something you can't help—ask your dog. Conditional love, on the other hand, is maintained only with effort, patience, kindness, and unstinting compromise. Am I saying that my wife's love for me wanes a tiny bit every time I am slow to take out the recycling? Yes, that is what I am saying.

Staying together has got very little to do with the vague promises you made on your wedding day, and a lot to do with adapting to conditions on the ground.

FOR POORER

As the twentieth century draws to a close, I find myself the father of three boys under five.

The youngest is born under circumstances that seem positively routine compared with our first outing. When I return to hospital six hours after the birth, my wife is dressed and ready to go, the baby packed up like hand luggage.

Initially, at least, there are few additional costs associated with the new baby. We already have all the stuff. Back at home I dig out our old baby monitor, only to find that it's made up of several mismatched components—parts accidentally swapped during group holidays and weekends away. After some experimentation I come up with a configuration of speakers and charging units that seems to work.

It's not much use as a baby monitor anyway, because the baby is in our bedroom with my wife, and most nights I'm dispatched to the spare room, where I am better situated to serve the nocturnal needs of the other two. This arrangement was not my idea. I don't object—I get marginally more sleep most nights—but I don't like the way it makes me seem. Having opted out of the ritual of exhaustion, I'm banned from grousing, or from conducting my life on an emergency timetable. And I'm still exhausted.

We mostly use the baby monitor during the day, when I sit in the kitchen making lists while my wife breastfeeds in bed and issues commands through the transmitter on her nightstand, next to the Moses basket, where the baby never sleeps. It is effectively a one-way intercom, allowing me to give free voice to unattractive thoughts. In the kitchen, no one can hear me complain.

"Nappies," says the baby monitor. Every list starts with nappies.

"The thing is, I'm tired too," I say, to no one. "I can't read this list, or feel my face."

"Onions," says the baby monitor. In the background I hear *The Jerry Springer Show* blaring from the bedroom TV.

"I've forgotten how to write 'onions,'" I say. "I'm going to have to draw a picture."

"Okay, let's bring out Brad," says the baby monitor, in Jerry Springer's voice. Brad's fiancée, it transpires, has a surprise for Brad. From where I'm sitting, it doesn't sound like a happy surprise.

"I wonder what it is that's made Brad so angry," I say, listening to the audience whoop for a while, forgetting who I am and how I came to be on Earth.

"Bin liners," says the baby monitor. I let out a long, theatrical yawn and write "bni larnz."

"Anything else?" I say. "I should go while I still remember how to drive."

"If you're just sitting there," says the baby monitor, "you could bring me some Twiglets."

"Yes, of course."

"We'll be right back after this," says the baby monitor.

There can be no paternity leave for the stay-at-home dad, because I have nowhere not to go to. Instead I just slack off for a few weeks, dodging phone calls, filing late copy, and writing with severely impaired concentration. Few of the publications I write for notice the difference. It is clearly possible to carry on working under these conditions indefinitely, so I do.

I have a small office in the attic, but I often have to come down and work wherever in the house I'm needed to provide minimal parental cover. My biggest skill as a stay-at-home dad is not child-rearing; it's being able to type while everyone around me is screaming. I'm hardly the primary carer (we have an au pair called Kate, so technically I'm the tertiary carer or, if you like, the parent of last resort), but I am such a domestic fixture that my oldest son actively disapproves of my going anywhere, as if it were a liberty fathers simply didn't take. He spends a fair amount of time away from home himself—at nursery, or swimming—but when he gets back he likes having me available for a lengthy chat about How Chickens Get Dead.

In spite of my stay-at-home status, I am occasionally required to leave the house. At the end of a rare three-day stint commuting to someone else's office, I come home to find the oldest one looking very disappointed indeed. He says he never wants me to go to work again, and I promise I won't. A few months later, when I tell him I have to go away for two days on an assignment (to Scotland, if I recall, to visit the set of a TV program), he starts rolling around on his bed, his little fists clenched in fury.

"Why can't you just write about this family?" he hisses.

There's a lesson there: be careful what you wish for, children.

The millennium arrives on the tenth anniversary of the night I first convinced my wife to kiss me. I forget to remind her of this when I kiss her again at midnight, at a big party in a big tent. It is not unlike that first New Year's Eve a decade before, in that we are both very drunk.

As a child I had once calculated the age I would be on January 1, 2000: thirty-six and a half. An immense sense of disappointment instantly swept through me as I realized I would be too old, decrepit, and joyless to appreciate the significance of such a huge event. My life would basically be over by then. Would I even notice the millennium?

To be honest, my prediction wasn't that far off. On a typical Wednesday afternoon in the year 2000, the Apocalypse could get under way without my noticing. I am pleased, for the moment, to be considered the primary breadwinner, because it gives me an excuse to stay in my office on the day that Music & Movement takes place.

When the local toddlers' music class got canceled, my wife decided to move the fixture to our house, arguing that it required no more than a CD player and a box of cheap rhythm instruments. It's still called Music & Movement, even though it's mostly Shouting & Crying, plus somebody's au pair hitting a tambourine. Even with my office door shut, I can feel it through my shoes.

At some point my wife also decides we need a dog. I disagree—it's my job to disagree—but I am not obstructive. I like dogs and I don't really see how more noise or mess will make a difference at this stage. I have adapted to the chaos; it's my normal working environment.

Theoretically, I can carry on like this indefinitely.

Except that 2000 is also the year the money runs out.

My career strategy until this point had relied entirely on the regular promotion of commissioning editors who like me. Several have moved from magazines into newspapers, then from one newspaper to another. The year before I'd started to write for the deeply understaffed *Independent* on Sunday, where I've since been made to feel indispensable. I write profiles and TV reviews and magazine features. I regularly get rung up to fill in for AWOL columnists at short notice, and I have two regular slots of my own. I barely have time to write for anyone else, which means I don't have to do the one part of my job I'm really bad at: casting around for more work. I wake up, change a nappy, drink a coffee, and spend the rest of my day with my nose pressed to the computer screen, making money.

Then there's a surprise change of editor, and I'm history, just like that. It's not a sacking, because I'm not on staff. I don't even have a contract. All I had was a lot of eggs in a single basket, and now I don't have that anymore. It's the sort of setback that all freelance writers face on occasion, but this is the first time it's happened to me. From one tax year to the next, my earnings halve.

At this point, my wife is not working at all. Our youngest child is still not a year old. For some years we have been living our lives at the very edge of our overdraft facility, and the sudden absence of a regular income tips us into dangerous territory immediately. For a while our marriage, which has stayed buoyant through repeated bouts of birth and death, looks as if it might founder over money.

Fighting about money is the worst kind of fighting. Money is freighted with associations—notions of power, control, success, status, dependence—so that when you fight about money, you're always fighting about something else as well. For this reason arguments over money are particularly unpleasant. They also last longer, and they're the most difficult to resolve: at the end of the fight, you still don't have any money. Studies have shown that financial disagreements between couples are a huge predictor of divorce, bigger than disagreements about chores or sex.

Before we ran out of it, I hadn't realized how rarely my wife and I disagreed about money. We never fought about spending or earning. We weren't extravagant. Money came, money went. Our financial affairs were managed calmly, if haphazardly. That was fine; neither of us aspired to be in charge. We lived, as many people do, a short distance beyond our means. But the mortgage was covered every month, and it seemed we'd learned to manage the perpetual juggling act. If we were pilfering small sums from the future, that was the future's problem.

However, in the time since I'd accidentally assumed the role of primary breadwinner, much has changed. Our division of labor has become, shall we say, a bit gendered. Because I can plausibly claim to be too busy earning, I'm excused a certain amount of parenting and general household bother. I never have to sit in a room with eighteen toddlers dinging a triangle and mouthing the words to "Nellie the Elephant." In my bid to prioritize work, I have begun to ignore the cat sick on the stairs.

By the time the money stops coming in I've begun keeping regular office hours, staying put at my desk, busy or not, until at least five p.m., so that I can arrive downstairs when my children are having supper, in a rough approximation of my own father's nightly return, when he would come in from the car and place his cold hands on the backs of our necks and we would squeal with delight.

"Get off, Daddy," says the middle one. I remove my warm, clammy hand from his collar.

"Look who it is," says my wife. "Your absentee father." She hands me a bowl of mush to post into the baby.

"How was school?" I say to the oldest one.

"Not fine," he says.

There are bills left out for me to see, bills with red stripes across the top. I know we don't have the funds to pay them, and I'm not exactly making a killing by pretending to be busy. I'm not fooling anyone, not even myself.

For two months I make the terrible mistake of waiting to see what happens. Nothing happens. Work does not magically come my way; my sudden disappearance from the world of freelance journalism has not caused a ripple. No one is saying, "Hey, whatever happened to that guy who used to write that thing sometimes?"

Discussions about what to do next are tinged with rancor.

"This is not about whose fault it is," says my wife, which to me sounds a lot like: this is your fault. My self-esteem plummets. I'm surprised how bound up my earning power and my self-worth have become; it's only been a few years since they'd been—out of necessity—completely decoupled. Now I'm starting to wonder how we ended up in the precarious position of relying on an idiot like me for financial support. Can I get away with blaming my wife for that?

My efforts to reestablish contact with former editors are answered by e-mails with vague promises in them. Nothing, I can see, is going to go right soon, certainly not soon enough to get us out of our growing financial hole. I begin to wonder if I can get my old day job back, which might well mean the end of freelance writing, which might well be for the best.

Fortunately my wife, who is weird about many

things, is not remotely weird about money. One of her greatest assets is her ability to separate financial issues from emotional ones, and to deal with the former with a certain brisk disdain. After several psychologically traumatic (for me) arguments about money, my wife decides that my complete failure as the primary breadwinner is, as far as she's concerned, an issue to be revisited later, at leisure, when I least expect it.

"Stop freaking out about your career," she says. "It's a bad patch, that's all. We just need to get some money from somewhere."

It is, she insists, a simple matter of a loan. Her readiness to incur more debt is, in an odd way, a tremendous vote of confidence; it demonstrates a willingness to gamble on future success. Unable to share her confidence, I settle for keeping my mouth shut.

So we go to the bank and borrow against our home for what I hope will be the last time (not even the second to last, as it turns out), and then I set about slowly rebuilding my tepid freelance career from scratch. In the meantime, I find myself available for a shitload of parenting.

SOME INDEPENDENT FINANCIAL ADVICE

• All the financial planning advice you will ever receive as a couple comes with an unspoken but implicit step one: First, Get Hold of a Bunch of Spare Money. If you have completed step one, the rest is easy. If you haven't, any subsequent advice is useless.

• If you do come across a bunch of spare money, and you also have a mortgage, then you should use all the extra money to pay down your mortgage. You probably won't, but you should at least give it some thought, if only so you realize that it isn't really spare money at all.

• The most important financial skill in any marriage is the ability to treat money—or more specifically a lack of it—as a common enemy. Don't fight about the money. Fight the money.

• Cede control where appropriate. It's simple: if you're stupid about money, then you need to defer to the person in your marriage who isn't. Earning more of the money, or all of it, shouldn't grant you any special influence over its dispensation. It's not your money—you're married.

• The priorities of family spending are remarkably straightforward, and should not normally leave you with leftover money to argue about. Knotty questions of pride, status, power, and independence are for people who have come across a bunch of spare money, in which case I should have your problems.

• If you're married, you need a joint account. An unwillingness to commingle your finances is, essentially, a reluctance to commit, and demonstrates either a lack of faith, a predilection for deceit, or a certain pessimism regarding the future.

• A periodic reckoning of where you stand financially is the best way to avoid a possible marriage-ending panic about debt. If your finances appear to be on a solid footing, including a comfortable savings cushion in case of future downturns or emergencies, check your figures. You've either forgotten something or you've added wrong.

IN SICKNESS

"It started four days ago, with a little sandpapery catch at the back of my throat," I say, pausing to examine my tongue in the bathroom mirror. "Then came the usual blocked nose; followed by streaming eyes and intense sinus pain. Yesterday, of course, was all about the chesty cough."

I am saying all this to myself, because my wife left the room as soon as I uttered the words, "I'm ill." She has no more interest in my symptoms than she does in my most recent dream.

"But now my throat hurts all over again," I say. "Which is weird."

In direct violation of the contractual clause that figures so prominently in old-fashioned wedding vows, neither my wife nor I has any patience when the other is in sickness. We have both developed a remarkable tolerance for illness in children—my kids are certainly the only people who've ever thrown up on me whom I've subsequently sought to reassure by characterizing the incident as no big deal—but our distaste for spousal ill health is unyielding.

There are a lot of reasons for this. Neither of us could be described as members of nature's nursing squad, nor are we model patients. Spouses often get the same contagious illnesses at the same time, generally from each other, so there's always the difficult question of where to lay blame. Malady is also a competitive arena, where men are said to cheat through exaggeration, while women possess certain genetic advantages: they are, for example, immune to man flu.

Make no mistake: this is a double failing, and a big one. When you see how much comfort a little sympathy, and a portable telly, can bring to a bedridden child, it's not hard to imagine what a fraction of the same could do for a marriage. Treating a poorly spouse with an attitude that could best be summed up as "I'll love you again when you're better" is not at all conducive to Gross Marital Happiness. In our house this indifference is not confined to the odd head cold.

I have the normal range of maladies for a man my age, plus a few so rare I've been obliged to name them myself.* I also have a bad back. At one time I thought of it as a mildly interesting part of my character, a Kennedy-esque infirmity that I bore with much stoicism and a certain amount of silent wincing. It seemed, if nothing else, a noble enough reason to excuse myself from a parents' evening: "My back's gone; sorry."

My wife does not feel the same way about my long-standing complaint. She thinks it's boring, and an unworthy topic of conversation. Whenever my back goes out she finds the timing opportune. If the problem persists for more than a day she grows suspicious, because it's impossible to determine the extent to which I'm exaggerating my symptoms.

"That rubbish needs to go out," she says, pointing to two full-to-splitting black sacks side by side on the kitchen floor. She can see that I am leaning over in the doorway like a flower with a bent stem, but she chooses to ignore my obvious incapacity. I haven't come down for tea and sympathy—just tea. In hindsight, it was a hideous miscalculation. After a long sigh, I shuffle toward the rubbish.

"I know your back hurts," she says. "Stop acting." She has always refused to accept that

*They include Phantom Phone—a creaking hip that makes me think my cell phone is vibrating in my pocket—and Cold Mouse Hand, which is self-explanatory.

extreme lower back pain comes with its own set of behaviors: walking with a hesitant, asymmetrical gait, head to one side, as if the room had suddenly tilted; sinking to one knee to retrieve things from the floor; frequent small grunts of pain, or louder gasps, if your wife is in a different room; an expression of deep uncertainty when rising from a chair. Of course I'm acting; on its own a bad back doesn't look like anything. If I didn't walk around the house looking like a depressed question mark, no one would know I was suffering. In terms of visible signs of distress, those stigmatics have it easy.

I turn and position myself between the two sacks. Squatting and grabbing them each by their slimy top knots, I attempt a straight-backed clean and jerk. But one sack is much heavier than the other, wrenching me into a painful posture. I can't help it—I yelp like a kicked dog.

"If you're in so much agony, why don't you go to bed?" says my wife.

"Because bed also hurts," I say, taking tiny steps toward the front door. "Besides, I can't go to bed. I've got business. I'm a businessman."

"You are not a businessman."

"I am a businessman," I say. "Presently one who has sharp tendrils of pain running up his left shoulder and across to . . ."

"I'm not listening to this again," says my wife. "La la la."

This is a common exchange, repeated between two and four times a year, depending on how regularly I do the back exercises I've been given. Then one day about fifteen years into our marriage, my wife hurts her back. She's not at home when it happens, but she rings me from wherever she is.

"It really, really, really hurts," she says, panting.

"Yes," I say. "I know."

When she comes home it's clear she's in considerable discomfort—she's hunched over and her eyes are watering, so I can't really accuse her of shamming. I think to myself: watering eyes—that's one I can use.

"When it first happened I couldn't stand up," she says. "It's like everything just went." I can't believe she's trying to appropriate my complaint. After years of being a banned topic, suddenly back pain is trending.

"This is just the beginning," I say. "Wait until tomorrow." For obvious reasons, my wife quickly loses interest in discussing her back with me. She rings friends who can offer undiluted commiseration, empathy without the taint of history. The next morning I overhear her telling one of them that it hurts more than childbirth. I briefly wonder if I am under any obligation to be the bigger person. Since when?

"I was talking about the very, very early stages of labor," says my wife.

"I knew what you were talking about," I say, "because I get those childbirthy twinges a lot."

"Shut up," she says. "Ow."

"Worse than childbirth," I say. "Childbirth plus." It is not my finest hour, although it certainly feels like it at the time.

The best thing I can say about our double failing is that it's a sign of a finely balanced inter-dependency; we need each other, present and correct, every day, in order to make life work. And since the intolerance is perfectly mutual, we manage to work round it—at least there is never any great debt of sympathy owed to anyone.

The impatience with infirmity toughens you up as well. I no longer talk about my symptoms in any detail. If I feel the need to communicate the extent of my unwellness, I tend to do it by asking loaded questions ("Do we have any painkillers?" "Is the ER busy this time of day, do you think?") rather than resorting to theatrics. It feels like progress.

IN FASHION

As a husband you assume an obligation—unspoken, unless it was in your vows—to dress in a manner your wife finds tolerable. How "tolerable" is defined in this context will vary considerably from couple to couple, but when it comes to avoiding the intolerable it is unlikely you will be starved for advice. And what is tolerable today may well be intolerable tomorrow.

This is the main problem with fashion: the rules change the whole time. While women's fashions cycle round with a reliable frequency—somewhere on the globe, someone is always championing the pencil skirt—men's fashions travel in a long parabolic orbit, like comets, and revisit less often. Certain unfashionable types of male apparel may not come back in style during your lifetime. I honestly thought this was true of hats. When I was thirty I assumed the hat was extinct.

As a rule of thumb men are always right not to trust a returning trend. If you were old enough to sport a particular look the first time round, you will be, by definition, too old to join in by the time it comes back.

I have never been fashionable, except perhaps for a brief period in the early '90s, when grunge was popular and all of us habitually sloppy people were accidentally swept into the vanguard. I didn't need to buy any new clothes for three years.

Wardrobe deficiencies should not unduly hamper a man's search for a partner. Women tend to be forgiving about a lack of fashion sense, although in what might be considered a primitive form of speed dating, a significant subset of womankind will instantly write you off for wearing the wrong footwear. This would not be a terribly difficult obstacle to surmount if there were some general agreement among women about which shoes were bad, but there isn't. My own advice is to exercise caution when it comes to dressing your feet: nothing too pointy, nothing too square-toed, too cheap, or too expensive; no innovative fastening mechanisms, no experimental materials, no colors beyond brown or black. Women will not, in my experience, get off on your blue suede shoes.

Footwear aside, a woman who likes you enough may agree to marry you in spite of your party shirt collection, on the unspoken condition that she shall subsequently be permitted to remodel you according to her own sensibilities. For her purposes a man who has no interest in fashion is preferable to a man with an assured sense of style that is, unbeknownst to him, horrible. Though there is undoubtedly something denaturing about turning control of your dress sense over to a woman, I advise you to surrender yourself to it at the outset. It's just easier.

For me it was not so difficult. Having moved continents, I was prepared to take on faith my wife's assertion that my American wardrobe did not travel well, and was, on some hard-to-quantify level, unpardonable. I often have to refresh her memory regarding the details of our first meeting, but not about what I was wearing at the time: "a bottle-green V-neck jersey over a nasty stripy button-down shirt." Needless to say, I do not remember this ensemble at all.

My wife was not herself a particular student of high fashion, and for years we both wore nothing but jeans and a series of interchangeable gray sweaters. Literally interchangeable: I often wore her clothes to work without realizing it.

Although I'm perfectly capable of choosing my own clothes, I also know that I can only wear a garment in defiance of my wife's disapproval so many times before I give in and retire it. And I do not like having to replace retired items, because I don't enjoy a minute of the time I spend buying clothes. I go to shops infrequently, often under duress, to pick up the thing I need most in the style I hate least as quickly and painlessly as possible. That's why I like shopping in airports—the selection is limited and the clock is always ticking.

This is not to say that I do not occasionally make mistakes. I have a special drawer for shirts purchased on a bold whim—a drawer I never open other than to remind myself that a foolish certainty is the hallmark of poor decision making. My most ill-advised attempts at self-expression are probably my Internet shoes, including an expensive pair that turned out to be much pointier than they looked in the picture on the website, and some too-large loafers I still occasionally wear when my wife is out. Frankly it's easier to buy love online than it is to buy shoes.

If I don't dress as badly as I should given my whole approach, it's because my wife supplements my wardrobe with purchases made on my behalf. The convenience of this arrangement is undeniable, although our tastes are not always perfectly aligned.

"Nice," she says, holding the neck of a cable-knit sweater against my Adam's apple. "Do you like it?"

"I'm not sure," I say, trying to weigh how much I actually dislike it against how easy it was to come by. "It's a bit, erm, textured, isn't it?"

"It's supposed to be like that," she says.

"I wasn't suggesting it was an accident," I say.

"It suits you," she says. I never know whether this constitutes a compliment or not.

"Does it?" I say. "Okay."

"You're welcome."

"Thank you," I say, although I'm fairly certain I will never wear it outside.

My wife's campaign to expand my wardrobe is nowhere near as concerted as her ongoing bid to rid me of about a third of it—the old, the holed, the stained, the faded, and the frayed. She's not interested in binning the old clothes I no longer wear, only the ones I do—my favorites—because I have worn them out.

Insofar as I have a fashion esthetic, it places no upper limits on the amount of damage a garment must endure to be deemed unwearable. Because I work from home it hardly matters whether my collars are frayed or my sweaters have elbows. I favor heelless socks and shirts with paint on them. The only thing I can't endure is a pair of trousers with holes in both pockets. No matter how much I liked them beforehand, once the pockets have gone, they're dead to me.

I wish I could maintain that my relaxed approach to dressing reflected an underlying self-confidence, but my lack of interest only serves to fuel my paranoia when I have to go places where my wardrobe might be judged and found wanting. For years I wouldn't even walk down Savile Row, for fear that someone with a tape measure round his neck would lean out of a window and shout, "Hey, pal! Gap's that way!"

To be honest, my interest in men's fashion only began when I started dressing my children. It is never lost on the fathers of small boys that their clothes boast both envious simplicity and effortless style. Toddlers can carry off blue shoes, even on the wrong feet. They know how to accessorize a dull ensemble by sticking a lollipop on the back. They dare to live by such bold maxims as "When in doubt, inside out" and they are entirely at home with the concept of asymmetry. Above all, they carry themselves with casual insouciance at all times. I once watched my middle son, then four, cinch up his too-big trousers by folding over the waistband until they were the ideal length.

"Did you invent that?" I said. He shrugged and turned his back, giving me a view of his front pockets.

"Actually, I think you've got those on back-ward," I said.

"It doesn't matter," he said. And he was right—it didn't.

It only works, of course, because they're young. Had I ever hoped that as my sons got bigger some sort of fashion cross-pollination—their effortless style joined with my money—would end up benefiting my wardrobe, I would have been sorely disappointed. When the oldest one eventually grew to be the same size as me, we did not, as a mother and daughter might, start swapping separates to fill out ensembles that mixed old and new, the safe with the daring. Instead all my white shirts disappeared overnight, commandeered without permission to supple-ment the boy's school uniform list. The next time I found one and put it on I noticed it had little cocks drawn all over the cuffs in blue pen. I'm afraid I can't carry that off with insouciance.

IN THE MIRROR

The seminal 1936 handbook *Do's and Don'ts for Husbands* retains, on most subjects, an admirable relevance. "Don't buy a motor cycle and side car without first consulting your wife," for example, is still timeless advice. Unfortunately the book is curiously reticent on the subject of grooming.

"Don't expect to be numbered among the good mannered if you use a nail file, comb or tooth-pick otherwise than in a dressing room" is about all it has to say on the matter. Wise as it is, this counsel doesn't quite address the modern phenomenon known as metrosexuality. For men, you will have heard, the stigma of taking pride in one's appearance has long since evaporated. It's okay to exfoliate. In fact, it's become a bit of a faux pas to let your skin stay on.

Let's not get too carried away. Half of men between the ages of eighteen and fifty-five may be happy to describe themselves as "metro-sexual," but the word itself is a fairly cautious coinage, an adjective that basically means "I live in an urban area and I'm not gay." It doesn't constitute an admission that you wear makeup to work. Men don't necessarily want to own up to being assiduous groomers, even if, as it is often claimed, we now are.

The evidence cited for this contention is an admittedly massive growth in the men's grooming sector: sales of men's skin-care products rose by £22 million last year, and the total market is worth something like £600 million. The top male moisturizer enjoyed a 188 percent annual sales hike. But this is not necessarily a sign that we are becoming more body-conscious, or measurably dandier, only that we are buying more stuff. Actually it's estimated that half of all male grooming products sold are purchased by women, so we're not even necessarily buying it. We're being gifted it, on birthdays and at Christmas, thanks to a national failure of imagination.

We're not so much exploring new territory here as going over old ground. At the turn of the twentieth century, men expended a great deal of time and effort on their appearance. Ordinary barbershop service often included a shave, a manicure, and the application of scents, tonics, oils, and unguents. When the Gillette disposable razor was introduced, self-shaving was marketed as a macho alternative to what advertisements called "the ladylike massage-finish of the tonsorial artist." A hundred years later, the ladylike massage finish is all the rage.

It could be that metrosexuality is not quite the revolution in body-consciousness we've been led to believe. In the US, sales of men's skin-care products actually dipped by 10 percent in 2010. Superdrug's Taxi Man line of male makeup (products invariably attracting jokey names like "guyliner" and "manscara"), launched in 2008, has quietly disappeared from the shelves. Almost a third of the men's grooming market is actually composed of shaving stuff. The bulk of the rest is shampoo, conditioner, and deodorant. The market is undoubtedly growing, but the simple fact remains that three-quarters of men over the age of eighteen still don't use any skin-care products.

Perhaps, like me, you remain metroskeptical; maybe you've purchased one or more of these products, possibly because you were feeling buy-curious.* Don't worry—I am not going to speak out against men using beauty products, because I have tried many—mainly women's beauty products. One of the advantages of being a husband is that you don't need to buy any creams, gels, or scrubs of your own—they're sitting there already, one shelf over, begging to be sampled. You don't even need to buy deodorant.

These products may not be packaged to appeal to men, but if, like me, you've ever been reduced to using a baby wipe as aftershave, you are probably well beyond the insecurity that prevents an adult male from buying moisturizer unless it's marketed as a hangover cure.

My bathroom cupboard contains two types of face polish. Both are made by the same company. One is intended for women, the other for men, the main difference being that the latter container is a manly brown. One was purchased by my wife, the other came from a goody bag I picked

---

*Of the two coinages in this sentence, I would most like to apologize for the second.

up at a party, even though the bag was clearly marked "David Walliams." Let Walliams buy his own face polish, I thought. There were some gin miniatures in there as well, which I drank in the taxi home. Anyway, the ingredients listed on both versions of the face polish are identical. They even smell the same.

It's probably a good test of the value of any male grooming product you're tempted to buy: is it so remarkably effective or confidence-boosting that you would happily purchase its female-targeted equivalent, the one with the butterfly on the label? Male vanity is nothing new, after all, and if you still won't countenance using a treatment that isn't disguised as a box of cigars, then perhaps you're not as metrosexual as you think you are. Fortunately for you, I have nothing to prove; I've tested many of these products over the years. Here are some of my findings:

- *Facial scrub.* Hurts to use. Doesn't really do anything—if you shave more than once a week, what's left to exfoliate?—and you end up with microbeads in your ears.
- *Under-eye repair gel.* Stings if you get it in, rather than under, your eyes. Doesn't repair anything. Occasionally handy for sticking down wayward eyebrow hairs, but this would be an expensive solution for such a chronic problem.

- *Anti-aging mask.* Doesn't do anything. At the end of the day, it's not even a very good mask—most people would know it was you.
- *Face polish.* Requires one to embrace the rather alien notion that it is desirable, even important, to polish one's face. Doesn't do anything.
- *Beauty serum.* No added beauty detected after several liberal applications. Wife no less beautiful despite mysterious disappearance of half the contents of tube.
- *Lift and luminate night cream.* Doesn't do either. No adverse effects if accidentally used during the day.
- *Tinted moisturizer.* Gives the skin on your face an even, "natural" tone, in the same sense that morticians use the word "natural."

While it's perfectly acceptable—from a gender parity perspective—for men to slather themselves in the same stuff that woman slather themselves in, we are still stuck with the troublesome fact that none of it works. No one is sorrier about this than I am, although I'll admit I take a certain pleasure in being the bearer of bad news.

The modern male is in the happy position of being alive in an age where the stigma associated with high levels of vanity (levels of vanity that have always, of course, existed) has faded, and yet none of us is actually required to adopt the new paradigm of grooming. Only one of the goalposts has moved. Our male cultural conditioning does not oblige us to take heroic measures against time and nature, to indulge in pointless expenditure, or to waste half an hour rubbing face polish into our cheeks and then blotting it off with a special cloth that costs extra. We are men; thanks to a lucky accident of birth, the beauty myth does not apply to us. Our skin is meant to be dry. We're supposed to look like shit first thing in the morning. Only a small fraction of the hair on our bodies falls into the "unwanted" category. Age is meant to wither us, and custom stale our infinite variety.

For decades this industry has made money out of women by trading on their insecurities, by commodifying beauty and setting unachievable standards for presentability. It's unfair, of course, but men won't help the situation by succumbing to the same con. We can treat ourselves to a wide range of notions of masculinity. We shouldn't have to buy any.

It's great that we live in a world where men can groom themselves to whatever extent they think is appropriate, from doing nothing at all to waxing your nuts weekly. I'm also aware that I may be safely to one side of an age divide—somewhere around thirty-three—below which men now routinely square off their eyebrows and go out in public wearing faces the color of tinted moisturizer. That's fine; I certainly don't want to put myself in the position of trying to stop young people behaving foolishly.

But before you ask yourself whether it's become acceptable to wear mascara, ask yourself if you can really be arsed. Men remain, compared to women, virtually maintenance-free, beyond a vague obligation to keep clean. This is your birthright. Think about what you'd be throwing away, in terms of dignity, complacency, and free time, by getting your chest waxed. I should know. I've had my chest waxed.

One of the more rewarding aspects of being a journalist is the opportunity to try everything once, if necessary with an outward show of reluctance, or an arm's length of ironic detachment, or even profound misgivings. It's why I once got into a shark cage for money. The list of male grooming interventions I have undergone, ostensibly so you don't have to (and also so I don't have to ever again), is long, and includes pedicures, manicures, facials, and the aforementioned waxing, which extended to the hair in my delicate umbilical region and is something I would never willingly endure again while conscious. Given the choice, I would definitely prefer another go in the shark cage.

I have endured a procedure which purported to tone my abdominal muscles through the attachment of electrodes. If you think running on a treadmill is a soulless pursuit, I'd suggest you try being hooked up to a machine that gives you stomach cramps on purpose. It would be cheaper, frankly, to drink a pint of old milk.

I have had makeup applied on several occasions, always while being assured that even up close no one would be able to tell I was wearing any. "It's literally just like an invisible gel," one grooming expert told me in the middle of one of these makeovers. For all I know, it came from an invisible bottle. If you told a woman her makeover was undetectable to the naked eye, she'd ask for her money back.

As far as I'm concerned, all these treatments proved either a complete waste of time or a woefully underpowered solution to an intractable problem. Trying to fix my feet with a pedicure is like trying to cure appendicitis with aromatherapy.

It's nice to be looked after, of course, and I'm sure many men endure pointless treatments on a regular basis simply because they like the attention. But after many years of sporadic prodding, primping, and pampering, I have learned two important lessons: a) I do not possess a sense of entitlement large enough to allow me to enjoy this sort of thing; and b) anyone who recommends tea tree oil as a remedy for anything is full of shit. Every cure we have today was invented because the tea tree oil didn't work.

15.

Do I Need a Hobby?

As a man you have probably had occasion to use the following conversational construct: "If you ever catch me X, then please feel free to Y," where X may be "building a model railway in my basement," "starting a pipe collection," or "reenacting famous battles at the weekend," and Y is either "shoot me" or "seek power of attorney."

I can only suggest you never put such a rash statement in writing. The fear of looking stupid fades dangerously with age, and without it, previously unacceptable pursuits can develop a perverse appeal. Getting older is, by and large, a process of rethinking all one's little rules about engaging with the world in order to see if there might be a pleasurable or satisfying pastime you haven't tried because you previously filed it under "would definitely make people think I'm a dick." This is not an old-man thing: the process begins well before retirement age. Fifty used to be the traditional threshold of unembarrassability, but these days we're seeing much younger men adopt uncool hobbies unironically.

A ruling passion is, in spousal terms, something to be tolerated rather than encouraged, because it robs a relationship of time, interaction, and money. There are, of course, many sidelines both husband and wife can engage in, but I'm going to insist that anything promoting togetherness has too much obvious benefit to be considered a hobby. One might argue that an established hobby is good for marriage because it's mentally therapeutic, but when a man insists his ten-thousand-strong moist towelette collection helps to keep him sane, we are right to question his understanding of the term.

So what is a hobby? Perhaps our definition would be enhanced by a further exploration of what a hobby isn't:

Reading is not a hobby. Reading is something you don't have time for anymore, *because* of your hobby—unless you're reading about your hobby, which doesn't count as reading.

Gardening is not a hobby; it's just outdoor housekeeping. Breeding hybrid orchids is a hobby.

Relaxing is not a hobby.

Exercising is not a hobby.

Going on the Internet is not a hobby. Everyone is on the Internet, always.

Gambling is not a hobby. Except for poker, and then only if you don't suck at it. Generally speaking, gambling is an addiction, while a hobby is a disorder.

Spending time with good friends, good food, and good wine is not a hobby. It's the opposite of a hobby. You need to get a hobby.

A hobby is not something you list in the "Other Interests" section of your CV, because a true hobby is something you would never want a prospective employer to know about.

Perhaps you don't think of yourself as the hobby sort. You may consider yourself a man of passing interests and ordinary recreations. And you may be right, but a mere pastime can, over time, become a hobby without your noticing. If you're worried, ask yourself these three questions:

1. Is your pursuit a banned topic of conversation at suppertime?
2. Have you ever felt obliged to lie to your spouse about how much money you spend on it?
3. When you tell other people about it, is their first question always "Why?"

I never thought of myself as a hobby person. I have trouble concentrating on one thing for too long, and I have a tendency to regard anything I'm not good at straightaway as stupid. When you have children there is no "spare time" anyway— only stolen time, robbed from areas of your life that are meant to be productive. On the whole I prefer to spend my stolen time staring into space.

Then one day I decide to make some sourdough bread instead. I'd probably once read an article about sourdough that made it sound easier to master than I now know it to be. But something about making bread without commercial yeast appealed to me. I could just use some of the wild yeast that's in the air all around us, and keep it in captivity. I'm often drawn to skills that sound as if they'll be useful in some post-apocalyptic landscape ("I am breadmaker, master of the yeasts of the air—please don't shoot me") although I'm rarely moved to act on such fantasies. There must have been absolutely nothing on telly that day.

Making bread also struck as a serviceably domestic indulgence: it would keep me in the kitchen, and could conceivably be counted as a form of household chore. I didn't make too many claims for it out loud, but I quietly figured a well-turned-out loaf was worth two loads of laundry.

It's easy enough to get started with sourdough. You just mix some flour and water in a bowl and leave it somewhere. In that respect it's a great entry-level hobby. After a few days the mixture gets a bit ripe and starts to bubble. There follows a cycle of feeding—more flour, more water—until the sourdough starter matures, expanding to the extent that you have to start getting rid of it. You do that by making bread with it.

My first sourdough loaf doesn't rise at all; it looks like a paving slab and weighs nearly as much. The second doesn't rise either. Nevertheless, for reasons which are not clear, I'm convinced I'm on the right track. It takes weeks of trial and error to come up with a loaf that my children can eat, but they don't like it. My wife keeps trying to talk to me about cleaning up the kitchen between failures, but all I want to talk about is bread.

I spend hours looking for help online, typing things like "sourdough loaf why giant holes" and "starter going weird help" into Google. I order special implements, DVDs, exotic flours, books, baking stones, and proving baskets. I tinker with the environment my wild yeast lives in, leaving explicit written instructions for its care when I have to go away. When I meet friends they ask me about my bread thing, because they know I have no other topics. For six months I turn out one troubled loaf after another, at the rate of about three a week. I estimate that in all that time I produced five loaves my wife and children actually liked and ate, loaves you might conceivably pay £5 for in a shop, provided you were told some of the money was going to a charity seeking a cure for whatever was wrong with the people who made the bread. I reckon they cost me £44 each.

At the end of the six months the urge to make bread suddenly leaves me. I think I must have eaten some really nice bread at a restaurant and thought, Why am I wasting my life? I cease all baking. The wild yeasts are left in the cold to perish.

"Can we throw that away yet?" says my wife, pointing to the moldering bowl of gloop at the back of the fridge two months later.

"I can't look at it," I say. "It's too sad."

"It's turned black, is all."

"If you must," I say. "I'll leave the room."

That was years ago now, but I've had a few bread relapses since—the dark days of January are particularly difficult—so I know I'm susceptible to hobbies. I keep watch for telltale signs of burgeoning enthusiasm, and I squash them.

On my forty-fourth birthday, my wife presents me with a banjo. This is a surprise for two reasons: 1) I knew she thought my having one was a bad idea; 2) she is not normally given to such extravagance in any case. The next year, she gave me a salad spinner.

She had known I wanted a banjo, though. I'd briefly held someone else's the previous Christmas, and became convinced that having one of my own would be the solution to all my least tangible problems.

It wasn't. I couldn't play the banjo. I didn't understand the instrument at all, and I found the beginner's instruction manual confusing and disheartening. I'd never even listened to much banjo music before and, on further investigation, I discover that I don't really like a lot of it. Two months elapse without any discernible progress on my part. I long to give it up. But I can't.

This is hard to explain. I've quit many things. I'm normally adept at coping with the self-reproach that comes with giving up. But I am kept awake at night thinking about the banjo. I become acquainted with all the many different styles of banjo playing, all of them equally beyond me. I spend a lot of time tuning it up, so it will be ready on the day I can finally play, although I am increasingly certain that day will never come.

It was clearly a mistake to invest the instrument with any sort of redemptive promise, but I still liked holding it, and most afternoons I end up sitting at my desk with a banjo on my knee, plunking away, and getting nowhere.

Eventually I discover a series of online instruction videos that start at the very beginning—a bit before the beginning, really—and proceed in small, idiot-friendly increments. I make halting progress, learning a simple song, then another, then another. When I look up from the strings, I notice that a year has passed.

I begin to sense that I am improving, enough to realize I have a long way to go before I can even consider myself bad. I decide I cannot make further progress without first buying a better banjo. Once I forsake her birthday present for a superior model, my wife relinquishes any obligation she might have felt about pretending not to hate my hobby. She lets it be known that the sound of it is like a curse that has descended on our home. I know what she means—even I am not completely immune—but I am undeterred.

Soon I am thinking about buying another banjo, one much better than my abilities warrant. I begin to lie about how much I am willing to spend, so that the actual outlay, when it comes, will seem a comparative bargain. My wife refuses to offer any opinion on the figures I present to her, hoping, I suspect, that my conscience will prevail. In the end the amount I pay is closer to my worst exaggeration than it is to my actual limit.

I still don't consider it a hobby. It's worse than that. I play the banjo every day. All day. It sits on a stand next to my desk so I can play when I'm supposed to be working. I just stopped to play it for fifteen minutes between this sentence and the one before it. In fact I wrote that last sentence solely as an excuse to play the banjo for fifteen minutes. For all the effort I put in, I really should be much better than I am.

It is an entirely private passion, unless you are one of my neighbors. It does not bring joy to those around me—quite the opposite—and it contributes nothing positive to my marriage.

I know the thing that bothers my wife most about my hobby is not the noise—though she dislikes this intensely—or the time it takes up, or the money I've spent. What really irritates her is the fact that I pursue it with a rigor that exists nowhere else in my life. I practice methodically. I look after my banjo with fussy precision: I always keep two sets of spare strings on hand; I have an extra bridge, various accessories (including a banjo mute, which I cannot recommend highly enough), and a collection of banjo tools neatly stored in the case. When it breaks, I arrange for its repair immediately. When we go on holiday, my primary concern is how—not if—I am going to get my banjo there and back. If the banjo doesn't fit in the car, then neither do I.

It cannot be pleasant to watch your husband rise to the occasion in a way that he always maintained he was incapable of, all for the sake of a hobby he didn't have when you met him. I have no excuses for my behavior, or any justification to offer. Unlike bread-making, in a post-apocalyptic landscape my banjo skills would get me killed, possibly after prolonged torture. I am sorely tempted to say that it keeps me sane, which is itself a deeply worrying sign.

16.

Fatherhood for Morons

At the outset of parenthood you may wonder what kind of father you are going to be. Don't worry: you are going to be your father, more or less. You may have long ago promised yourself you wouldn't emulate certain questionable parenting choices ("I'll never lock MY kids in a car while I watch an entire baseball game in a bar!"), but your disciplinary scowl, your strategy for tuning out those parts of a conversation that make no sense, and your habit of telling instructive stories from your past in which you figure as a terrible moral coward, all these will be based directly on your dad's child-rearing techniques. You won't even have to think about it; it will just happen. It's not your fault—you've only got the one role model, if that.

Or perhaps not quite just one. Some people don't grow up with full-time fathers, or even part-time fathers, or even fathers, but those of us who did still looked further afield for supplementary role models who seemed more progressive, more patient, and more at home in the modern world where we would eventually come to live as grown-ups. They might be the fathers, or the much older brothers, of school friends, or even faintly groovy teachers. Most of my off-site role models came from television, and even then I cherry-picked, ignoring the typical TV dad's eagerness to punish dishonesty while still admiring his propensity to book vacations to Hawaii.

My father, however, remains the primary template. Every father-son experience is, in some sense, a son-father experience relived, with the roles reversed and the script unchanged. When it came time for my oldest son to learn to ride a bicycle, I turned it into the sort of rite of passage from which neither party emerges with much credit, simply because that's how I remember it. That way I could make direct comparisons, improve on my father's performance, and thereby contribute in some small way to the great sweep of human progress. I would show myself to be trustworthy: if I promised not to let go, I would not let go. I would not allow myself to run short of patience or let it show if I did. It would not be a frustrating, bruising experience. Not this time.

The bicycle is the boy's most prized possession, a reward for learning to swim, even though he hasn't learned to swim. By this time I've given up on swimming, fully intent on leaving all future instruction to professionals. But I don't think you can hire someone to teach your kid to ride a bike.

For six months I've pulled him around the park by a rope wrapped round the handlebars. He does not pedal, although he occasionally squeezes the brake once we've got going, in order to pull me off my feet. His balance is not good; whenever we take a bend he leans toward the outside stabilizer, and the bike lists alarmingly. Even after six months, the bike is still a bit big for him. He is apprehensive in the saddle and, like his father, prone to panic. Unfortunately, he is also persistent. He does not get this from me. I don't understand why we can't just give up, like we did with swimming.

Eventually I untie the rope. I tell the boy I'm going to push from behind so he can learn to steer himself. He doesn't like it. He repeatedly tells me to slow down, even though we're proceeding by inches. I'm beginning to admire my own forbearance, which is, I have since come to realize, a bad omen. He pedals apprehensively as I jog along behind, applying constant forward pressure to the seat to stop his grinding to a halt. Twice he accuses me of letting go. I repeat my promise, but when my back starts aching from stooping and pushing, I do let go. He is about eight yards ahead of me when the bicycle drifts to the edge of the paved path. He tries to correct himself with a sharp left turn and—this is with the stabilizers still on, remember—tips the bike over. He spills onto the grass and lets out a bloodcurdling scream. The other people in the park turn toward the noise.

"I hate you!" he shrieks as I pick him up.

"It's fine," I say, righting the bike. "You're fine."

"It's not fine!" he shouts, tears jetting from his eyes. "Willy-man!"

My wife laughs when I tell her the story, but I don't laugh recounting it, or when I think about it later that night. That he felt moved to invent a term of abuse—to coin his own approximation of "dickhead" using the vocabulary available to him—in order to make plain the intensity of his lack of regard, is deeply wounding. I want to apologize, to beg forgiveness, to admit that I basically deceived him when I implied that learning to ride a bike would be a fun and pain-less experience, because I knew he'd never attempt it if I told him the truth. But I have a stronger urge to say nothing, to carry on teaching as I was taught. I convince myself that it's never too early for a child to learn that a father is someone who lets go when he says he won't, because his back is weak and his patience is thin.

His grim determination means we are out in the park the next day, trying again. I am very much on the back foot on this occasion, a proven liar whose advice cannot be trusted, whose every instruction is picked apart.

"I know it seems odd," I say, "but you need to

lean the other way, in the direction you're turning."

"Of course that won't work," he says.

The next time he comes off the bike I cannot resist the temptation to tell him it was because he didn't listen to me. The argument that ensues is protracted and vituperative and ends with my picking up his bicycle and throwing it into a bush. It's not my proudest moment as a father. I wish I could say it was my unproudest moment, but there are several others vying for the distinction.

We take a long break from bike riding, the boy and I, while I reformulate my plan and probe my memory further. I recall that it was my mother who was there with me the day I finally learned to ride a bike, on a cold and windy morning in the empty beach parking lot. I don't know whether my dad had officially forsworn our bad-tempered and unpropitious lessons, or whether he was just at work. I do remember a sense of urgency: my sixth birthday was looming, and everybody I knew could ride a bike.

The knack of riding a bicycle is, like any skill, a product of all that accumulated failure, but I only remember the moment when I felt the bike holding itself up of its own accord as I pedaled maniacally and my mother's encouragements grew faint. I didn't see her expression, because I never looked back.

We return to the park many weeks later. My wife is there with us, enabling us to deploy that most last-ditch of all parental strategies: the two-pronged assault. I have not asked for this, but I think she has sensed the reinforcement is necessary. As long as she is there to second my advice, to echo my stilted praise in slightly different words, then the boy's objections to my tutelage are effectively neutralized, and he knows it. He will not call me "willy-man" today.

He's also a little bit older, his legs a little longer. To my shame, I realize that when I first bought him the bicycle he was barely four. I'd been acting like a victim of the child's persistence, when the pressure originated entirely with me.

I've taken the stabilizers off the bike and lowered the seat as far as it will go. By degrees his mother and I get him to accept that if he feels the bike tipping he can just put his feet down.

Running along bent over while holding the back of his seat is absolutely punishing, but the boy is making progress. When, by mutual agreement, I let go at the appropriate speed, he doesn't look back either, not even once. You can't really. If you look back, you just fall off.

AUTHORITY

Before I had children I imagined them chiefly as an outlet for my didactic impulses. I'm not a natural teacher, or a particular fount of wisdom, but I still have a strong need to divest myself of information as and when that information occurs to me.

This is not the same as being good at it. I tell a story the way I would write one—beginning far too early in the proceedings, including details that turn out not to be germane, returning frequently to earlier points in the narrative to effect minor adjustments, pursuing discursive sidetracks in order to include facts I happen to know, and editing on the fly by instructing my audience which bits of what I've just said to disregard. I get there in the end. Unfortunately the listener, unlike the reader, is not presented with a product, but with a process.

When a gentleman imparts knowledge to a woman in this manner, it is sometimes known, disparagingly, as "mansplaining." It's considered both sexist and patronizing, but it is the normal way of conversation among men—to go on and on about something you are pretending to know a lot about, pausing only when someone with a louder voice starts talking over you. Above all, one must never risk asking a question. It might well be the last thing you say all evening.

To use this mode of discourse on women is not always intentionally patronizing; in many cases it is simply boorish, a failure to take into account the fact that your interlocutor is someone other than your brother. Men speak to other men as though they're always about to be cut off, because they probably are. In my younger days I remember panicking when I spoke to women and they let my stream of chat run unchecked as if it were some kind of lecture. "Why isn't she interrupting me?" I would think. "I'm almost out of words, and this anecdote has no ending! Oh Christ—she's not actually listening, is she?"

But my kids—they won't know any better. They will listen to my undifferentiated spume of digressive memoir, rhyming aphorisms, and historical misinterpretation as if it were the Gospel. I won't have to tailor my didactic nature to suit anybody but me. The answers I provide for their questions will be taken as scientific fact. But I had not reckoned on the questions.

"When are you going to die?" asks the oldest one, age three. I pause thoughtfully, pretending it's a question I had never before considered.

"Oh, not for a long time," I say.

"Yeah, but WHEN?"

He's not much older when he leans forward in his car seat one day—after a long, contemplative silence—and says, "Mumma can never escape from us, can she?"

"Sorry?" I say.

"Because we could just follow her wherever she goes," he says. It's always tricky to answer a question when you strongly suspect your interlocutor of possessing more relevant information than you. What does the boy know that I don't? Has she got plans to move towns and take a job at the local library under an assumed name? Or is it just something he imagined, or dreamed, or saw on TV? What sort of reply could cover all these eventualities?

"Mumma can run," I say. "But she can't hide."

I also imagined that along with my wisdom, my very bearing would command a certain innate respect, a natural awe that I should probably offset rather than encourage so as not to become a distant, authoritarian figurehead. I deliberately cultivated a benign, nonintimidating presence from the outset, more family dog than father, although I began to distance myself from that persona once we got an actual dog. I thought of my future role as approachable, collegiate, instructive. I reckoned that as they grew my children's respect would be a natural by-product of my inspiring example. I even dared to imagine my own little audience following me around laughing a bit too eagerly at my strained jokes; it would be just like hosting *Loose Ends*.

What I did not foresee was a day when, while interviewing a newly demobbed *Apprentice* contestant in the course of my work, I would flip through my notebook in search of an incisive question I'd jotted down earlier, only to come across a page on which the words "DAD YOU

SUCK" had been written in two-inch-high block capitals with a black marker.

I did not envision a time when, during one of my lectures about manners and public etiquette in a noodle bar, my children would take turns poking chopsticks into my ears, until the theory that I was possessed of a sense of humor about myself had been comprehensively disproved. I did not imagine that the oldest one would develop a habit of greeting me by slapping me lightly on both cheeks, or that the middle one would hijack my Twitter account in the night to post heartfelt admissions of loserdom ("Hi, I suck at everything I try in life") or that the youngest would insist on addressing me as "Daddy me laddy."

Episodes like these prompted some questions of my own: When did I graduate from caregiver to figure of fun? Why is it so amusing to prick my pomposity? At what point did I actually become pompous? If I were being charitable to myself, I would probably argue that I am partly complicit in my children's efforts to undermine me, that on some level I'm even abetting it, because sons in particular need an opportunity to distance themselves from a father's authority even at an age when they remain obliged to acknowledge it. But that's not what I'm doing; I never even thought of that. I'm just making them laugh, and not on purpose. And as they get older, I just seem to get funnier.

Is it to do with my personality, I wonder, or is it something about the times we live in? I have a sneaking suspicion that my self-importance may be in some innate way self-sabotaging, if only because I suck at everything I try in life. But I also know that when I was a child grown-ups were more or less exempt from ridicule.

In the winter of 1974 my father walked into a glass wall at the Hilton in Pittsfield, Massachusetts. He was striding across the deck of the indoor swimming area, wife and four small children trying to keep pace with him, past a neat line of deck chairs toward the hotel's poolside restaurant. He was attempting to slip between two occupied tables when he hit the glass at full speed—this particular panel was missing the eye-level *H* decal that marked out the two flanking it—much to the consternation of the diners on the other side.

My father was knocked to the ground by the impact. I remember him crawling around on his hands and knees for what seemed a long time, dazed and unable to grasp what had just happened to him.

"For Christ's sake, Bob, get up," said my mother.

"I'm trying," he said as blood dripped from the end of his nose. He was fine after a few minutes, but we did not eat in the hotel restaurant that night.

I try not to think about how my children would react if something similar happened to me, but I know from bitter experience that they do not hesitate to laugh when I slip on ice, or when I'm being questioned aggressively at passport control, or when I'm freaking out about data loss, or being on the wrong motorway in Italy, or when I object to having chopsticks inserted in my ears in public. Were I to walk into a glass wall, I sometimes think their only regrets would be about not having the presence of mind to film it.

No one laughed when my father walked into the glass wall at the Hilton in 1974; it wouldn't have occurred to me. Mind you, I didn't feel a tremendous amount of empathy either. I was too busy feeling guilty, because I'd known the glass was there all along. I'd spotted the illusion on an earlier foray to the lobby that afternoon, and had been vaguely planning some stunt to fool my family. For that reason I was pleased we were heading right for it; I just hadn't reckoned on my father getting quite so far ahead of me. I never intended for him to walk into the glass, but there was a discernible moment when I realized he wasn't going to stop, and I still chose to say nothing.

I felt terrible about the incident for years afterward, but I never admitted the truth. I figured God would get me back for it someday. Perhaps, at last, He has.

SPORT

My biggest recurring worry, once I realized I was to be the father of boys, was that I would let them down when it came to the question of sport. After twenty years in Britain I still can't do enough football chat to last through a whole haircut. My father's enviable record of sporting achievement and dedicated spectatorship was not something I could look to for guidance; he didn't know anything about soccer either. I was flying blind.

After a lot of private fretting, I decide to approach the eldest shortly after his birthday. I begin my little speech with all the caution of a man who suspects he's already left something important too late.

"Now that you're eight," I say, "we need to make a big decision."

"I'm nine," he says.

"Yeah," I say. "So we need to decide which football team we support."

"What are you talking about?" he says.

"It's traditional, I believe, for British sons to inherit some form of allegiance to a team from their fathers, but since I don't have anything to pass on, I thought we could look at . . ."

"We support Chelsea," he says.

"What?"

"We're Chelsea supporters."

"Since when?" I say.

"Since always," he says. I have no idea what "since always" means to a nine-year-old, but I'm not really in a position to dispute the contention.

"Oh," I say, a little disappointed. "How are they doing?"

"They're fourth, but they have a game in hand."

"I see. Can you just quickly explain what that means?"

That was it—an issue I'd worried about for eight years was solved with one two-minute conversation. If only all of fatherhood were so simple. But it turned out nothing else of it was that simple.

My children were not raised in a sport-spectating household, but they live in one now, a universe entirely of their own making. I do my best to join in: every year when the football season starts, I make another doomed attempt to cultivate a knack for commentary. I know the rules, but I remain incapable of making intelligent remarks during an ongoing match. I can't tell the players by their numbers, or their positions. When the referee blows his whistle I rarely know why. At some point in the second half I invariably say something that betrays my failure to realize the teams have swapped ends.

"Why is he passing it that way?" I shout. "What the hell is wrong with . . . Oh, I see. Nothing."

One Sunday evening in October I walk into the sitting room to find the middle one watching a game. I sit down beside him, looking in the direction of the television without really taking it in, letting the commentators' meaningless blather wash over me.

"What's the score?" I ask.

"Ten–seven," he says.

"Really?" I say, leaning closer to the screen. "That's an unusually high . . . hang on. This is *football* football. American football."

"Durhh," he says. Great, I think: here is a sport I actually understand, sort of. This is the game of my people! Quick—what would my dad say next, if he were here?

"Who's playing?" I say. A safe enough opening. I don't want to overplay my hand. I mean to wear my lifetime of knowledge lightly.

"The Jacksonville Jaguars and the Houston Texans," he says. I cannot, alas, allow his simple error to go uncorrected. He'd do the same for me.

"There's no such team as the Jacksonville Jaguars," I say.

"Yes, there is," he says. "Look!"

"Well, I've never heard of them," I say. "They sound made-up. And Houston are called the Oilers."

"No, they aren't," he says.

"I think you'll find they are," I say. "Because of, you know, all the oil."

"When did you last watch an American football game?" he says. I think about my answer for a moment.

"Twenty-two years ago," I say, "or thereabouts. But there certainly wasn't any . . ."

"Dammit!" he shouts at the television, exactly the way my father would.

"What's happened?"

"Penalty," he says.

"For what?"

"Taunting," he says. "Fifteen yards."

"Taunting?" I say. "Since when can they penalize you for being a dick?"

"Shush!" he says. "Just watch."

The Houston Oilers, I later learn, moved north, and eventually changed their name to the Tennessee Titans. In 1999.

Throughout parenthood—usually when you're on your knees with exhaustion—older people have a habit of coming up to you and saying, "Enjoy it—it goes by so fast." And they're right—it does go by fast. Just not at the time.

In the thick of it, parenthood seems neverending, its compromises deep and permanent. In a few short years I have gone from being appalled by the low hygiene standards of small children to being appalled by my own low hygiene standards.

I had always imagined that my children would

at some point graduate from being charges to being minions—that I would be able to assign them tiresome chores or dispatch them on small errands in exchange for their upkeep. It would be like having an army of tiny personal assistants.

This never really came to pass. It's true that for the promise of fifty pence a six-year-old will look for your glasses all day, but he will not find them. An eleven-year-old will not look, not even for a fiver.

I spend most of my time in search of their stuff, or fulfilling their demands, or coping with the fury of someone whose maths homework won't disgorge from the printer because of a connection issue that is somehow my fault. It turns out that parenting is a lot more like being a personal assistant than having one. In fact, it's a lot like being Naomi Campbell's personal assistant, but without the travel.

Up close this time of dirt, tears, insolence, and missing gym shorts doesn't feel like something one should necessarily cherish. From a distance it may resolve itself into a fuzzy, happy-family tableau, but I'm not sure how far back you'd have to stand.

Pat, the man who introduced me to my wife, who was best man at my wedding, is sitting in our kitchen and laughing at us.

"Take that out of here!" shouts my wife at the younger two, who are fighting over a deflated football while the dog barks.

"I could not live like this," he says, laughing. Pat is single and has no children, but because of his hand in our partnership he regards our day-to-day existence as a vast, picaresque misadventure laid on for his amusement. He drops by most weekends to see how it's progressing.

"Get off!" shouts my wife at the cat, which has jumped onto the worktop to sniff the butter.

"Your cat has no tail," says Pat, laughing.

"I told them I didn't want the tail," says my wife, climbing onto a stool to swat the little worms that have been migrating across the ceiling all week, northeast to southwest. They're coming from somewhere in the store cupboard, but I have been unable to locate their exact point of origin. The oldest enters with wet hair.

"Where are my shoes?" he says.

"They're probably where you left them," says my wife.

The football bounces into the kitchen, knocking a mug off the table. Pat laughs. The younger one chases the middle one through the room and out the other door.

"I'm going to kill those two," says my wife.

"I need my fucking *shoes*," says the oldest, stomping out.

"How can you live like this?" says Pat, laughing.

"Only with the tireless assistance of my helpmeet here," says my wife. I look up from the newspaper to see that she is indicating me with an oven glove.

"Sorry?" I say.

For the most part parenting is, as in the above example, a shared activity, but I tend to think of fathering as that fraction of parenting that I do on my own, when my wife is working, or when she insists that a week in Majorca will only be a holiday for her if the rest of us don't come. It gives me a chance to measure my child-rearing skills against a baseline of competence, and the opportunity to speculate on what it would be like to be a solo, full-time parent.

There is, of course, nothing remotely heroic about a father's looking after his own children—especially not the way I do it—although when it happens in public I still sometimes feel I'm being watched as I were some kind of absurd novelty, roughly equivalent to a monkey smoking a pipe. Again, that could have something to do with the way I'm doing it. But there is no question that the bar has been set very low for fathers. You can show up at the school gates in your emergency glasses (one earpiece only) with hair like a bonsai elm, toting three kids flecked in breakfast, minus one lunch, and nobody says a thing. You can pick up in the same outfit in the afternoon, you can be late, and you don't have to bring cupcakes. To be a father out there, on your own, is to present a direct challenge to the notion that parenting is some kind of competition sport.

"We had a good day," I say to my wife on our return from an afternoon out. "Except for him. I shut his thumb in the car door."

"You what?" says my wife, examining the oldest one's swollen, navy-blue digit. "Why did you do that?"

"It was an accident, not a punishment," I say. "Gimme a break."

This lone parenting most often occurs in the course of my normal fatherly duties—an over-ambitious supper cooked in my wife's absence, a load-lightening cinema excursion, the odd school event I have to do on my own, the kind of Saturday outing where I lie about where we're going until everybody's in the car—but occasionally it's touched off by my saying something rash out loud.

"A music festival?" I say one fateful evening. "Yes, of course I will take you to a music festival."

Perhaps it's because my children are boys, but when I'm on my own with them in public I'm often conscious of setting either a good or a bad example. I'm worried they're learning how to be men from me, or worse, that they're just learning too much about me. I've always been gratified by the extent to which my children have not taken after their father—they seem fairly confident, easygoing, and at home in the world—so I try to limit their exposure to the sight of me operating outside my comfort zone. The problem is that most things worth doing lie outside my comfort zone. Back in 2007 a music festival struck me as the sort of managed environment where not too much could go wrong. That's probably because at that point in my life, I'd never been to one.

It's already dusk when I arrive with the older two, having squandered valuable daylight hours in standstill traffic a regular festivalgoer would have known to expect. What I had expected was some sort of system for transporting our gear from the distant car park to the festival proper that didn't involve me just carrying everything. There isn't. They do have a system for taking my two bottles of red wine off me at the gate, though.

"No glass," says the gatekeeper.

"How convenient," I say.

"You can either drink it here or leave it here," he says. This is precisely one of those instances where I'm conscious of setting an example. I can't down two bottles of wine in front of my children. What about one bottle? Half a one?

"Hang on," I say. I shrug off all my baggage and pull a full one-point-five-liter plastic water bottle from my rucksack.

"Drink," I say to the oldest. "Drink a lot." I pass it to the middle one and command him to do the same. I take a large swig and pour the rest on the ground. The two bottles of wine fill it to the brim. They're not the same kind of wine—they're not even from the same region—but the situation warrants desperate measures.

"I'm pretty sure we can buy more water once we're in there," I say. "Let's go find out."

By the time I've managed to trudge to a space that will allow me to put up our tent—a £69, two-pole monstrosity with the footprint of a bouncy castle—it's too dark to see the nettles that are clearly the only reason this particular patch of ground is still available. My children lie on all our stuff, arms folded, while I offer a running commentary that I hope will prove mildly instructive.

"First, we peg out the bottom of the inner tent," I say as the middle one shines a torch in my face. "Then we take tent pole number one, and . . ."

As I bend to retrieve tent pole number one, something like a cello string snaps in my lower back. I make a strange, involuntary sound, and as I jerk upright I jab the tip of the tent pole through the fly sheet, tearing a six-inch, L-shaped gash. I turn to see my two children staring at me as if I were an insufficiently diverting repeat of *Red Dwarf*. A light rain begins to fall.

In the morning, I can barely move. A night in a sleeping bag on a slope has done nothing good for my back. The sun is blazing as I shuffle, crabwise and listing slightly to port, in the same direction as the streaming crowd, my two children ahead of me.

"We need to stay together," I say. What I mean is: don't leave me. The festival has four main stages, a number of smaller tents, a vast array of foodstuffs, even a special children's area, but it lacks the one thing I am desperate for: a chair. There is no sitting down to be done anywhere; there is only standing up and lying on the hard earth.

We walk the festival from end to end, alternatively listening to music and eating food. My wife's hostility toward my bad back is nothing compared to my children's cold indifference. They ignore the sudden, sharp intakes of breath and the quiet swearing. They consult the schedule, then the site map, and then they start pulling my arms.

"Ow!" I say.

"This way!" shouts the middle one. "It's starting."

I jostled by crowds and struggle to cope with uneven grounds. Under the weight of the ruck-sack that contains our stealables, my twisted frame contorts further; one of my shoulders rises up to touch my ear. By the middle of the afternoon, however, I realize that I'm not going to die of a bad back after all, because I'm going to die of exposure first. We all are.

"We must have hats," I say. "Find hats."

After scouring the site for suitable headgear we choose two trilbies and a porkpie hat from an overpriced stall. It makes me smile to see my children in stupid hats, until I remember I am wearing one too.

It is after midnight when we finally get back to the tent and I can lie flat and suck on my giant wine bottle. Both boys are hyped up and in no mood to sleep. They are not the only ones. People are playing drums next to my head.

When we finally get home the next evening my wife insists on the usual debriefing session following any foray where I'm in sole charge.

"What was the worst bit of all?" she says, eyes shining.

"Definitely the end," says the middle one. "When we had to pile all the stuff on Dad and lead him to the car like a donkey."

"I could carry," I say. "I just couldn't bend."

"He was so slow," says the oldest. "It took ages."

"What was the second-worst bit?" says my wife.

"Do we have any painkillers?" I say. "Would the ER be busy right now, do you think?"

Life does not fly by when you're trapped at a festival with a bad back, or stuck in standstill traffic on the M5, or listening to a child play "Moon River" on the violin for the 230th time.

But this stage does end abruptly: before you develop any sort of knack for dealing with it, it's over.

Suddenly you find yourself looking at photos on a pin board: three boys, arranged by height, sitting on a bench with an apple apiece; a moon-faced eight-year-old in a stripy sweater, holding a kitten; two brothers arsing about at the top of a sand dune. They look just like your life, until you compare them to the hulking creatures rolling fags in your kitchen.

It's true what the old people say—it does go by fast, and you'll miss it when it's gone. But you shouldn't feel too guilty about letting these years breeze past you. If you try and savor them, they just go by faster.

At least once a week my wife is wont to declare, without prior consultation, that "tonight's supper is free-range." "Free-range" does not, in this sense, refer to the dignified and highly ambulatory life of the chicken that gave its withered left breast to tonight's edition of Spicy Ricey. "Free-range" in this context means "you can take your food and go wherever you want with it, provided it's nowhere near me."

No one in our house has ever objected to a free-range supper. I usually take my plate and a brimming glass of wine and sit in front of the television. I might be joined by a child or two, but they usually head for the computer, or the Xbox. I think the youngest one sometimes eats his supper in the bath while watching a movie on a laptop—an indulgence I find objectionable for many reasons, but have also vowed to try one day. My wife eats in the kitchen, alone and at peace.

The shared meal is the very center of our family life, which is probably why we have so many methods of escaping from it. "Today's lunch," my wife will sometimes announce, "is silent reading only." A range of newspapers and magazines is provided, but diners may also bring their own books, or even laptops. Everything is permitted, except talking.

Sitting down together every night was not necessarily part of the original parenting plan. When the children were tiny they ate separately from us, but over time their supper hour got later while ours got earlier, until the two merged into a single, problematic sitting. As a meal the shared supper more or less succeeds—everyone sits, everyone eats—but as a social occasion it leaves a lot to be desired. As a proving ground for civilized dining, it's positively counterproductive.

Conversation is by turns bad-tempered—"Why are you being such a dick?" is a routine, if officially proscribed rejoinder—and exuberantly inappropriate. The youngest usually makes a bid to leave the table before I've even sat down.

Catastrophic spills are common, and fights sometimes break out. Meals embarked upon with the best intentions occasionally end with my wife saying, "You're all horrible," and walking out.

I wish I could say that the family lunch becomes easier to stage as the children get older, but it actually gets harder. Teenagers fight among themselves more. The swearing only gets more baroque. With each passing year, everyone learns to eat a little faster. I never imagined I would pine for the days when the youngest two were still in high chairs, and spent the entire meal delicately applying food to their faces like makeup.

I'm not saying I do not enjoy a chaotic Sunday lunch, because I do. I have a reserved seat at the end of the table, so for once I feel nominally in charge. The children aren't usually in a rush to be elsewhere, because they've usually just got out of bed, and the meal gives me a chance to catch up with their business. As someone who rarely leaves the house other than to walk the dogs, I find the recounting of an ordinary school day fascinating, especially if they do the teachers in different voices. I have a particular fondness for stories about people being arrested on the bus, and I am rarely disappointed on that score. When this avenue of inquiry has been exhausted, I enjoy hearing a brief summation of my children's weekly achievements.

"What's the best thing that happened to you this week?" I say, indicating the youngest with the tines of my fork.

"I missed maths because of a fire," he says.

"Well done," I say, turning to the middle one. "What about you?"

"They read out my tweet on the poker channel," he says.

"You must be very proud," I say.

"I recorded it on my phone," he says. "Look."

"No phones at the table," says my wife.

"I'm finished," says the youngest.

"No, you're not," my wife says.

"Pass the salad," I say.

"You're the salad," says the middle one.

"Ah," I say. "Touché."

I'm sure I will miss these days once the children excuse themselves from the table in order to move to Australia, but at the moment the best thing about a big Sunday lunch is that it means Sunday supper is automatically downgraded to free-range.

TIPS FOR A SUCCESSFUL FAMILY MEAL

• Where possible, don't limit it to family. Sunday lunch with other people invited is much easier, provided you can get other people to come. The presence of non–family members has an eerily civilizing effect on adolescent boys in particular. And the presence of other children helps to dilute the bad behavior of yours.

• Contrary to my wife's opinion, you cannot curtail a graphic dinner table discussion about newsreaders vomiting live on air by introducing the topic of homework.

• Sometimes the best time for a family meal is a day when the whole family is not present. Partial gatherings are usually more successful, and removing one child from the equation always makes things go more smoothly. I don't know whether family meals are more harmonious in my absence. I don't give a damn how they behave when I'm not there.

• You can cram a lot of togetherness into twenty minutes. Children do not, as a rule, like to linger over meals, and consider any non-eating time spent at the table to be a form of imprisonment. Obviously manners, discipline, and a parent's tiresome need to make a point occasionally require a child to stay in his chair longer than he might care to, but if you get a quarter of an hour out of him, you're doing well.

• Introduce new recipes and exotic foodstuffs only on free-range nights and at silent reading lunches. It takes children some time to acquire new tastes, and you don't want to hear anybody's opinion the first time.

17.

Keeping the Magic Alive

My wife and I do not say "I love you" to each other every day, or even once a month. I don't begrudge couples who do, but I would like to put in a good word for the ones who don't. It can't be the end of the world, this failure to be consistently demonstrative, and if your relationship—like mine—is partly founded on a shared distrust of the falsely effusive, it's hard to invest any faith in the power of some snuggly incantation.

I personally believe there are lots of ways to express one's feelings that don't rely on those three words uttered in that exact order on a regular basis. It's perfectly possible to replicate the gist of a commonplace exchange like "I love you" and "I love you too" using slightly different language. In our house, for example, we prefer "You'll be sorry when I'm dead" and "I know."

Unfortunately, nothing I have read about maintaining a happy, healthy relationship supports my position. All the tips I've absorbed over the years have stressed the importance of making an effort, of saying the actual words out loud and forcing oneself beyond the embarrassment that comes with doing anything out of the ordinary for the first time. Almost every prescription for upholding romance mandates ritual reinforcement, regular doses of affection, and the constant transformation of positive regard into demonstrative behavior. It's invariably presented as difficult and time-consuming work. "We have a myth that love should be easy," a relationship counselor once told me when I had the temerity to complain about the effort implied by his advice. "Love is a skill; you have to learn it and practice it."

I still want love to be easy, and for that reason I am terribly susceptible to any method that sounds as if it might constitute a shortcut. This was what first attracted me to a newspaper article suggesting that four hugs a day is the secret to a happy marriage. I know from experience that my wife is suspicious of unscheduled displays of affection, but written down like that, four hugs just didn't seem like that many.

"Four hugs a day," I say as my wife tries to squirm her way out of hug one. "I think it's the way forward."

My approach for hug two, just before lunch, is from the front—moving in slowly, arms low, palms showing, approximately the technique you would use to take a picnic basket away from a bear.

"Thank you," says my wife, petrifying under my touch. She doesn't seem to be responding positively to the treatment, but that's okay. One of my favorite aspects of the quick-fix prescription is the total lack of nuance, subtlety, or follow-up. The newspaper article doesn't suggest alterations to the technique in the event of a poor outcome. It just says "four hugs." I find I'm even beginning to enjoy her irritation a little. It doesn't matter whether she likes it or not. I win either way.

"Already?" she says when I move in for hug three at about sunset.

"No one said this was going to be easy," I say.

When it comes time for hug four she is nowhere to be found. I know she's home—the car is out front—but eventually I give up looking. I blame my lack of persistence for this particular strategy's failure.

A week or so later I read about something called "whisper therapy." There isn't much information about the technique—it's only mentioned because Madonna and Guy Ritchie are said to be using it to save their marriage. Apparently it involves a lot of eye contact and the regular whispering of certain positive sentiments to one another. It sounds incredibly annoying and, for that reason, I can't wait to try it.

I'm not quite sure how to proceed. I don't know whether Guy and Madonna have preselected and mutually approved the words they whisper to each other, but that seems wrong to me. It ought to be more spontaneous than that.

Things get off to a bad start. When I steal up behind my wife and whisper, "You are special," in her ear, she hits me over the head with the hairbrush she is holding.

"What the fuck are you doing?" she shouts.

"Whisper therapy," I say. "Ow." I don't cite the *Grazia* article where I first learned about the technique, because I don't think it will help her understanding of its underlying principles.

Over the next few days my wife grows eerily patient with my habit of leaning over at odd moments to whisper things like "Nice shoes," "You're magic," and "Kind to animals." I think she is in denial about the therapy's awesome power to annoy. I increase the stakes, whispering in her ear when guests come round, to make it clear we are the sort of couple who still share romantic secrets.

"He says he can't wait for you to leave," she tells them.

"Not really, though," I say. "It's just a thing we're doing. More coffee?"

A week later Madonna and Guy Ritchie split up, and I call off the experiment. I'm not necessarily suggesting that whisper therapy destroyed their marriage; I just suddenly realized that the only people who resort to crackpot therapies like this one are people whose marriages are all but unsalvageable already.

Some months later my wife and I enter a phase

where we periodically jab each other in the neck with two fingers, accompanying each strike with a short, sharp hiss. We learned the technique from watching *Dog Whisperer*, and it began as an efficient, no-nonsense way to clear someone from your personal space, or get their attention if they seemed not to be listening. But over time it became a mildly painful form of affection, and then thankfully, it got old.

Eventually, and largely for the sake of writing a few thousand words on the subject, I convince my wife to attend actual couple's counseling. It is, in the words of our counselor Andrew G. Marshall, more of a "marriage checkup," but that doesn't make the prospect any less nerve-wracking. Although ostensibly nothing is wrong, we're still making an appointment for a routine examination that could possibly end with us being told our marriage is in a serious condition. This is, after all, what sometimes happens with a real checkup.

On the way to the first session my wife and I concoct a few problems for Marshall to solve, which is a bit like making up sins to confess so you don't have to tell the priest what you've really been up to. This scheme quickly falls apart—even if you intend to treat it as a journalistic exercise, you can't spend three hours in a room with a marriage counselor without some genuine issues coming to light.

The take-home message from our three sessions is that my wife and I speak different "love languages." She relies on "caring actions"—i.e., doing everything—to demonstrate her love, while I tend to concentrate on clumsy affection. Our problem, it seems, is that we would both prefer to be shown love in the manner we are accustomed to showing it. I am prescribed a course of caring actions: unsolicited aid; spontaneous-sounding praise; small, thoughtful presents. My wife is put in charge of clumsy affection. We continue to fail in this, albeit with a more solid understanding of what we are doing wrong.

At the peak of the publicity surrounding the 5:2 Diet—the one where you fast for two days a week, and do what you like the other five—I am commissioned to write a piece about using the same on-again, off-again formula to revitalize your marriage. My wife, a devotee of the 5:2 Diet, is intrigued by the prospect of only being married to me two days out of seven, until I explain that it's not how it works—for two days a week we will be extra-married. Of the multipronged program set up for us by our former marriage counselor Andrew Marshall, the only bit I really practice with any regularity is the sending of romantic texts. On the two nonconsecutive days we attend to our marriage, in between texts that read "pick up booze" and "What printer cartridge do i need," I slipped in a few saying things like,

"I appreciate everything you do." I know that's not terribly good, but it's actually my first go at being saucy.

More recently I came across a range of intimacy exercises so powerful they are said to be able to make strangers fall in love. Once again I zero in on the easiest of the lot: a few minutes spent facing your partner, with your flat, extended palms as close together as possible without touching one another. The power of this exercise is undeniable—my wife can only stand it for a few seconds without shuddering with something that looks, to the untrained eye, like revulsion. Such is its power to annoy that for two weeks I insist on having a go every time we cross paths.

My findings on these quick fixes are twofold: none of them really works on its own, but taken together, they sort of do. If marriage teaches you anything, it's that there is value in the occasional lame gesture and half-assed experiment. It shows you're trying, and eventually one builds up a little repertoire of rituals that come in handy during those occasional periods when the strain of being together makes easygoing affection hard to come by.

18.

Head of Security

If you were to ask me what, as a husband and father, keeps me up nights, I would answer straightaway: it is the night itself. Nothing brings me more constant, unrelenting anxiety than the obligation to protect my family from unknown, unpredictable harm, the kind that swirls up from the darkness—or occasionally drops from a clear blue sky—without herald. It's not really anxiety —it's just plain fear: the fear that I'm not up to the job. Or more precisely, the *knowledge* that I'm not up to the job. Were the position vacant, I certainly wouldn't hire myself to fill it.

It's not that I am insufficiently paranoid. Whenever I see my children enjoying themselves, my mind begins to enumerate potential hazards. And for every potential hazard I can conceive of, I have a corresponding, gruesomely detailed imagined outcome, all because I spotted a sharp edge and said nothing. So I say something.

My wife has a name for me that she deploys whenever I start fretting about having more car passengers than seat belts, or I insist that sharp knives are loaded into the dishwasher points down. She calls me Mr. Health and Safety.

That's what she called me at that drinks party where the host had just proposed to light the two dozen or so candles decorating her Christmas tree. I was in the middle of making an unpleasant little scene, and ignoring criticism from several guests who said I was being kind of a downer.

"Have you ever heard of a candlelit Christmas tree not catching fire?" I shouted.

"I think you're being a bit paranoid," said someone.

"Have you met my husband?" said my wife. "Mr. Heath and Safety?" I made no apologies for my reaction then, nor do I now. Because of my tireless, swivel-eyed insistence, the candles stayed unlit, and thirty people were spared the prospect of dying like characters in an Edith Wharton short story. My children weren't even there; I was just trying to keep them from being orphaned.

I wasn't always this way. I have a history of personal recklessness. Once, on coming home without keys after a night out, I climbed the facade of my apartment building in Boston with a knife in my teeth to slit the screen of an open second-story window. I don't suffer from any debilitating or unattractive phobias; I don't much enjoy being in the same room as an uncaged bird, but I can cope.

I do, however, suffer several disorders on behalf of my children, the most crippling of which is acrophobia-by-proxy. I cannot watch them hang over balcony railings, or gambol on clifftop coastal paths, and I will not share anything described as a viewing platform with them. They're the ones who stick their heads through the bars to spit on the cars below, but I'm the one who gets the vertigo: my heart pounds, my palms sweat, my vision undulates. When they were little I used to hold them by their shirt collars whenever we had to use a pedestrian bridge. Now that they're teenagers they won't permit this, but the urge, I assure you, has not left me.

I still remember the feeling of panic that came over me watching the youngest crawl around on the glass floor of our London Eye capsule, and I still get dizzy recalling our two-day visit to the Grand Canyon. I can't even look at the photos.

Although my antennae are always attuned to danger, real and imagined, that is no cause for anybody to feel secure in my presence. I could go round saying I'd do absolutely anything to protect my family, but I have a rough idea of what I'm capable of, and I know perfectly well it isn't good enough. All the time I've spent looking anxiously out of windows, or fretting late into the night, or crawling through playground equipment with one hand gripping a tiny ankle, or standing on the shore, scanning the waves and counting heads—these have amounted to no kind of vigilance at all. Keeping my family safe and well is largely a matter of hoping circumstances will conspire to keep my limits untested.

And for the most part, they have. But not without some notable exceptions. Occasionally that nameless dread that keeps me up nights takes on hard edges, rears up in my face, and tells me its name.

In January 1998 the oldest one, who had just turned three, developed a high fever over a number of days. Our GP took one look at him, stabbed him in the thigh with a massive injection of antibiotics, and told my wife not to wait for an ambulance, but to drive straight to hospital. By the time she got in touch with me she was hysterical, having had to beg a stranger for his parking space so she could carry a listless toddler through the doors of the emergency room.

"What do they think it is?" I said.

"Suspected meningitis."

I was holding the middle one at the time, who was ten days old. He couldn't go to the hospital and my wife, who was breastfeeding, couldn't stay. As soon as the oldest one was admitted we swapped places. I spent three nights on a mat next to his bed, while a nurse came every hour to note his vital signs and check the drip that ran into his arm, secured with bandages and a splint so he couldn't pull it out. It was the first time I'd felt that peculiar combination of terror, powerlessness, and a very bad back, but it would not be the last.

• • •

In November 1999 my wife woke me to say that she'd heard a noise.

"What kind of noise?"

"Like a bang," she said. "From downstairs."

I got up and walked to the landing, from where I stared down into the blackness and listened. After five minutes I went back to bed. Only when I woke up in the morning did I notice the splintered front door hanging loosely from a twisted dead bolt. Although the perpetrator did not ultimately gain entry, he did manage to destroy one of the most expensive things we owned: our front door.

My wife called the police. I went and had a bath, where I spent a long time thinking about the risk an intruder might have posed to my family, and my failure to investigate a noise even to the extent of turning a light on, because I was sleepy. By the time I got downstairs a policeman was examining trainer prints on the outside of the door.

"Here's the have-a-go hero himself," said my wife. I tried to explain that I was guilty not of cowardice, but of a total failure to grasp the situation. In the cold light of day it sounded a rather lawyerly distinction.

"I would have done the same thing myself, sir," said the policeman, but we both knew I hadn't done anything.

When the youngest was a newborn I left him asleep in his pram in a fish shop, completely forgetting that I owned an infant. I then walked half a mile to a playground to meet my wife, without it once occurring to me that I might be missing something. I was still wondering how to explain my decision to purchase two dozen goose barnacles to her when she looked at me and said, "Where's the baby?" I was lucky. I know for a fact that no one in that shop would have batted an eyelid if a sweaty, panting, furtive-looking oddball had suddenly burst through the door and run off with a sleeping infant, because no one took any notice when I did it.

On a beach in Cornwall the following summer, the middle one, aged two, toddled behind a rock formation and tipped soundlessly into a deep pool, conking his head on the way down. At the time I had my back to the sea and was busy trying to get my towel laid out just so. The first I heard of the incident was when a stranger with a wet child in his arms started shouting, "WHOSE BABY IS THIS?"

Not long after that, the youngest one was rushed to hospital with a high fever. Once again, my wife rang me from the hospital.

"What do they think it is?" I said.

"Suspected Kawasaki disease."

By this time the Internet had become quite a thing, and there was no need for my fears to be contained by the limits of my imagination: within seconds I was reading a terrifying list of complications. Fortunately the hospital where the child was lying listless and feverish was Britain's leading treatment facility for Kawasaki disease. Even more fortunately, he didn't have it. But before we found that out I spent another sleepless night on a hospital floor, trying to find the words to ask a God I simultaneously feared and didn't believe in for help.

On the morning of July 7, 2005, when bombs were detonated across London as my children were on their way to school, I was on a train to Paris with a bunch of sandwich-board signs with French slogans ostensibly designed to console Parisians over their loss of the Olympics to London the previous day, or, if you like, to rub their noses in it. I was meant to march around the city with them strapped to me, front and back, in order to attract as much opprobrium as possible. So much did I regret accepting this assignment that I'd spent most of the previous night wishing a disaster would arise to prevent my carrying it out, although to be honest I was thinking of something more along the lines of a small fire in the Channel tunnel.

A month later a nail bomb was discovered in the park across the road from where we live, having been dumped there a week previous by one of the more reluctant July 26 bombers. I spent the next forty-eight hours of enforced indoor living—while policemen with machine guns patrolled the pavement—trying to reassure my children that the world was still a non-terrifying place, basically by shouting, "Look! Our house is on TV!" A week after that, when we discovered that the bombers were more or less our neighbors, I employed the same tactic: "Look! Our house is on TV again!"

One night the following summer I was awakened by a loud noise I could not square with the deathly silence that followed. Can you dream a noise loud enough to wake you? While I was considering the possibility I fell back asleep. In the morning I found the front window wide-open, and everything portable of value—money, credit cards, laptops, phones, iPods—missing from downstairs. I realized we'd been robbed by the sort of burglar who wants you to be home—he's after the stuff you take with you when you go out—and is probably prepared for the possibility that you might wake up and raise objections. I was rather grateful to have slept through the whole thing. It saved me having to make a difficult moral choice between cowering in fear and getting beat up.

Not long after that, my oldest son reached the age where boys start getting mugged by other boys on their way to and from school. The other two soon followed. As a father I find few things more upsetting than having to hear these regular tales of confrontation. For a child there are few things less useful than advice rendered after the fact. I'm never quite sure what to say anyway.

As someone who spent the better part of his childhood poised on a continuum somewhere between fear and embarrassment, I am perhaps not in the best position to offer tips on how to cope with bullying and intimidation. There's only one instructive story from my past I ever trot out for them, and I don't actually come out of it very well.

When I was twelve I got cornered by a larger boy—although my age, he was six inches taller, with a dense beard—between two rows of lockers after gym class. He walked over and rested a giant foot on the bench where I was sitting. "You," he said. "Tie my shoe."

At first I pretended not to hear, and continued getting dressed. When he repeated the words, I looked up as if I had not realized he was speaking to me. Then I affected not to understand the exact nature of his demand. I acted as if it were merely rhetorical, an insult requiring no action from me other than to seem a bit hurt. Then I pretended to assume the demand was actually a generous offer that I was, alas, too humble to accept. Then I admitted—as if this were the real secret I'd been trying to hide all along—that I was really bad at tying laces, and that he was better off seeking help almost anywhere else. I expressed all this haltingly, sometimes drifting off in midsentence while I did up a few more buttons on my shirt. Eventually a bell rang, a gym teacher strolled by, and my tormentor lost interest in me as a victim.

"In the end it doesn't matter what you say," I tell my children. "The point is, you must never tie the shoe."

They're not remotely impressed by this little parable, and much prefer the story about my being punched to the floor in the hallway by a girl the previous year. My wife doesn't think either tale has much of a moral.

"If someone wants to steal your phone, you give it to them," she says. "It's just a phone. It's not worth it."

Actually, would-be muggers have so far always rejected their phones for being too shit, so they really aren't worth it. Even so, most of the time my sons just lie and say they don't have a phone, while never slowing their gait, and this usually suffices. They're probably in the best position to know the difference between a bit of speculative bullying and a genuine mugging, and how to behave if one suddenly becomes the other. They're out there every day, after all. It's nothing to do with me, but I like to think they know exactly when a phone is just a phone, and when handing it over would be tying the shoe. I hope so because, although I hate to admit it, they're on their own out there. It's a sad fact of fatherhood that by the time your children are old enough to need it, all your advice turns to dust in your mouth. The opportunities to provide protection from the world diminish daily, or so I imagine.

In the autumn of 2009, on the afternoon half term started, the oldest one, half a dozen of his friends, and his youngest brother went to the park over the road with a football. When I next looked out an upstairs window an hour later, they were playing a jumpers-for-goalposts-style match with some other kids who happened to be out there. With the sun setting, it looked from where I stood an idyllic scene. When my wife called me back to the window half an hour after that, things had changed.

"There's something going on out there I don't like," she said.

Evidently the game had ended, or was ending, in dispute. In the charged, not altogether wholesome half-term atmosphere of the crowded park, other kids were streaming over to take sides. Even from a distance, it was clear that my son and his friends could count very few well-wishers among them.

By the time I got outside (I spent a long time looking for my shoes, half hoping the situation would resolve itself) everybody was gone. The oldest one, the youngest one, and the oldest's friends had sought sanctuary in the corner shop at the park's edge, where upward of thirty other children—most of them quite young, it has to be said—had gathered outside. More were arriving all the time, drawn by a sense that something was happening. When I arrived they were all busy looking bored, but there was a definite crackle in the air, a palpable sense of menace held in abeyance. It was like that playground scene at the beginning of *The Birds*.

Before I could go in, a clutch of nervous boys in white school shirts stepped out of the shop, the oldest at the back, and headed down the pavement for home, an evening stroll of less than a hundred meters. The crowd of children turned as one to surge after them, and I fell behind. For a few moments I was in the uncomfortable position of being part of the mob following my children.

As I picked my way to the front I could see that they were doing the right thing: walking slowly and deliberately, ignoring the front row of the mob, who were diligently kicking them in the calves as they went. But I also realized events might well come to a head before we reached the front door. In my mind the unknown thing I had lain awake so many nights dreading—a scenario which promised an unpredictable combination of fear, failure, and embarrassment—had arrived. My big test as protector, the one I was beginning to imagine I'd dodged, was here. I had no idea how I was meant to deliver us from the situation, but the time of intervention, it seemed, was upon me. I held my breath and took one large, final step forward.

I was still more embarrassed than angry, given my strong disinclination to put myself in any position where I might have to address a large group. I insinuated myself directly behind my children, turned so I was facing the mob, spread my palms, and said, "That's enough." I'm not sure they heard me at the back. The mob continued to press.

"You can't fucking touch me!" said a kid at the front.

"They're my children," I said, lamely. Any illusion I might have harbored about having a lot in common with Atticus Finch as played by Gregory Peck deserted me at this point.

Just as I was beginning to regret my lack of prepared remarks, a boy of about fourteen rode up on his bike, hopped off, pulled his hoodie tight over his face by the drawstrings, and punched me in the mouth. I experienced a soundless, frozen moment. A car stopped in the middle of the road and the driver opened his door. I touched my mouth and looked at the blood on my fingers. The boy got back on his bike and rode off, without my ever grasping the nature of his involvement. The crowd evaporated. The driver got back in his car.

"Let's go," I said. I led the children back to the house in a calm, unhurried fashion.

Another parent who heard the whole story told me I'd done the right thing, but I don't recall making any choices. I touched the spot where my tooth went through my lip and thought: at least you didn't have to give any sort of speech.

For a time, I treated this incident as the ultimate squaring of the demands of fatherhood with my personal fear and embarrassment thresholds: painful but necessary. I figured I'd done what I could in the circumstances, had been found wanting, and yet it had all worked out in the end. With some relief, I decided to let this serve as parenting's worst-case scenario.

More recently, however, a chunk of ice about the size of a beach ball fell from a cloudless sky and crashed into an artificial pitch where my son was playing football. I was standing on a Tube platform when I received this news, and two tears escaped my brimming eyes as I stepped onto the train, even though I'd also been told he was unhurt.

I called him when I got off the train and he explained that the ice chunk had landed right in front of him and exploded on impact, whereupon a tennis ball-sized fragment had flown off and hit him in the chest. The other players were racing up the pitch at the time, while he, having just disappointed himself in defense, had dejectedly paused to tie his laces. The ice, he said, had probably broken off an airplane, although I later learned that the Civil Aviation Authority disavowed this theory, cataloging the event as an unexplained icefall of the kind that were reported long before the advent of commercial air travel.

I think it upset me so much because, in spite of twenty years of hand-wringing, hyperventilating, and health and safety paranoia, the incident reaffirmed my conviction that the fundamental experience of fatherhood is one of bottomless responsibility alloyed with total impotence. You spend eighteen years holding on to collars, patrolling the beaches, strapping on seat belts and helmets, purveying tiresome homilies, and inventing new dangers to worry about. And then one day ice falls from the sky. It's hard to be "there" for your children under those circumstances, but to be honest I'm glad I wasn't standing on the touchline when it happened. Who knows? I might have shouted at him not to tie the shoe.

19.

Misandry—There's Such a Word, but Is There Such a Thing?

One of the greatest things about being a man is that you come with a certain level of empowerment as standard. If you're a white, Western, straight male, you tick virtually all the empowerment boxes. Even if you can't lay claim to the full slate, you've still got a decent head start. While you may experience some lack of empowerment from being a minority, or because you suffer from one or more unattractive phobias, being a man—just by itself—leaves you remarkably unencumbered by the need for self-validation. Any path in this world not open to you because of your maleness is . . . wait—there aren't any! All right: you can't give birth, a privation which, for my money, is a lot like someone denying me the right to bungee jump from a helicopter. I'll cope.

Given the way the world currently works, it's almost impossible to discriminate against men for being male. Or is it?

I recall some years ago watching *The X-Factor* with my children, and being obliged to explain the difference between sexy and sexist.

"Sexist," I said, "is being prejudiced against someone because of their gender. But actually, only women."

"Is that true?" asked the oldest one.

"Well, I can't think of an example where it works the other way round," I said. "Can you?"

"Yes!" he shouted. "Sheilas' Wheels!"

This was a cause of his at the time. Adverts for Sheilas' Wheels insurance were all over the telly—we'd probably just watched one—and he felt very strongly that offering discounted car insurance exclusively to women drivers amounted to a gross injustice.

"That's slightly different," I said. "The simple fact is . . ." I stopped there, because as a father I have always reserved the right to abandon sentences that have no future—kids forget these conversations instantly anyway. I realized that simple facts didn't come into it. As far as I knew, there was no written rule about when one's basic human rights could be trumped by actuarial tables. I had no idea how we as a society came to accept that certain bonzer car insurance deals could be off-limits to men simply because statistics proved they had way more accidents. And being sexist against men—that wasn't even a thing.

The boy, it transpired, was right, or at least not alone. The European Court of Human Rights subsequently ruled that car insurance premiums have to be gender-neutral. So effectively women drivers are now required to subsidize accident-prone males through higher premiums. But that's not fair either. There is no "gender-neutral" position to take on this ruling; it's sexist either way.

Of course, one might simply blame men for being such terrible drivers. Personally, I'm not going to lobby on behalf of my gender over something that we, as a group, ought to be ashamed of. Maybe we can't help it—perhaps it was a sudden surge of testosterone brought about by the act of purchasing shelf brackets that caused me to drive into the bollards in the Homebase car park—but to be honest, the idea that I could be unfairly treated just because I'm a man has never occurred to me. And I'm always looking for new reasons to feel hard done by.

Recent years have seen the rise of two novel terms: "masculism" and "misandry." At first glance they seem to spring from nothing more than a tit-for-tat desire for lexical fairness: there is misogyny, so there must be misandry; we have feminism, so we might as well have masculism.

It's fine to have the vocabulary at hand, should a need ever arise. But where is the need, unless you're desperate to use "sexism, but against men" as a crossword clue? Is not the world as we know it, as we have always known it, already a giant lobbying group for men? Who calls himself a masculist? Why? In opposition to what?

In February 2013 the Twitter hashtag #INeed MasculismBecause began circulating, encouraging men to enumerate the injustices that made men's rights activism such a timely necessity. As a parody of the popular #INeedFeminismBecause hashtag, it had all the hallmarks of a "calling all morons" piece of provocation—and the hashtag was quickly appropriated by Twitter users who deployed it to illustrate the absurdity of the whole notion of masculism. "#INeedMasculismBecause women have had it too good for too long" was a typical example. My favorite ended ". . . just because I'm handsome doesn't mean my name is 'handsome.'" Even the sincere tweets were difficult to distinguish from parody: "#INeedMasculismBecause the American feminist movement fights for superiority not equality."

#INeedMasculismBecause was, in fact, a deliberate attempt to troll feminists. There were no actual masculists involved in its creation—some sexists, maybe; some dickheads, certainly—but nobody who really believed that men needed a movement to further their struggle. The windup was itself a derisive parody of masculism, constructed to provoke a feminist reaction against contentions nobody was making.

If the hashtag achieved anything at all, it served to reinforce the notion of men's rights activism as an online backwater where angry losers who can't spell "privilege" complain about having to pay for dinner all the time. It certainly did the trick for me. You won't catch me calling myself a masculist.

Mind you, I don't often call myself a feminist either, if only because I don't think I could turn up to a meeting without someone pointing at me and shouting, "What's HE doing here?" I'm a man—a small cog in the patriarchal machine—and therefore part of the problem. Back in the 1970s, when a male sitcom character said something like "Speaking as a feminist myself," we were being asked to laugh at his wishy-washy liberalism; now we would probably laugh at his hypocrisy. When a male politician is asked if he's a feminist, he will never have a short answer. If you pinned me up against a wall and asked me if I considered myself a feminist, I would probably say yes, but I would be very worried about any follow-up questions you might have: What feminist things have you done lately? Why haven't you done more?

Additionally, a lot of feminism's current battle appears to be with itself—the media is full of feminists telling other feminists that they aren't real feminists, or that feminism no longer means what it used to mean, or ought not to mean what it presently means. While I find all of this truly fascinating, gripping even, I know it's not my fight. When it comes to the vexed question of what needs fixing about modern feminism, nobody is asking my opinion. And if women are struggling to qualify as feminists in the eyes of other women, I'm certainly not about to jump the queue.

So while I'm happy to be counted as a supporter, to uphold the basic tenets of feminism and, where relevant, to retweet them, I couldn't start a sentence with "Speaking as a feminist" any more convincingly than I could say, "Speaking as a small-business man." Both might be true by somebody's generous and inclusive definition, but I'd only be fooling myself in the end.

Conversely, I am only nominally a member of the patriarchy, the male-dominated social system against which feminism struggles. Let's put it this way: they don't send me their newsletter, and if they have a Christmas party, I've never been invited. For all the advantage the patriarchy has conferred upon me because of my gender, I strongly suspect the bastards are still holding out on me. As far as I can tell they appear to be running the world for the exclusive benefit of people who own more than one helicopter.

This is, of course, an oft-cited reason for men to seek common cause with feminists: the patriarchy is fucking with us too. Men don't necessarily refer to the overarching system that runs the show as "the patriarchy" among them-selves. We just call it The Man. And while I admit to being a man, I don't tend to think of myself as

The Man,* so from my point of view a men's movement that was allied with feminism, against The Man, would be, in theory, a cool thing.

The trouble with the men's rights movement (MRM) is that it's mostly—actually almost exclusively—an antifeminist movement. It seeks to lay the problems facing the modern male at feminism's door, which is simply not my experience. I can't think of anything bad that's happened to me that I can blame on feminists. Robots, yes; feminists, not really.

The MRM is also largely—and perhaps fortunately—an Internet thing, confined to drab corners of cyberspace most of us never visit. It's sometimes collectively described as the manosphere, which makes it sound pretty inclusive, but it doesn't appear to include very many happily married men. In fact it's largely an online refuge for aggrieved ax-grinders who tell anyone expressing a positive view of modern gender relations to "keep taking the blue pills."

---

*Though I fully accept that I am The Man to an extent, in that I benefit from the patriarchy even as I am being disadvantaged by it, and that I am almost certainly coming out ahead in comparison to other genders, sexual orientations, and socioeconomic groups, and probably at their expense as well. This, I think, is what I'm being asked to bear in mind whenever someone tells me to Check My Privilege, an unfortunate imperative to which I always long to respond with the words "Make me."

Unless you haunt the right online forums or follow a particular subset of people on Twitter, it's unlikely the concerns and provocations of the men's rights movement are keeping you up at night. They certainly aren't talking about misandry down at the corner shop, and you don't have to read too many blogs about First World governments controlling the masses through "aggressive gynocentrism" to see why.

Men's rights activists (MRAs), one soon discovers, aren't even particularly concerned with helping men. They don't tend to build, fund, or even campaign for domestic violence shelters for men; they just keep pointing out that there aren't any, even though there are loads for women (thanks to feminists), in what amounts to nothing more than a point-scoring exercise. Men's rights activism isn't a cause; it's just a hobby for misogynists. Their primary concern appears to be able to complain, apparently without a shred of irony, that men are the real victims of victim culture.

They don't necessarily mean all men either. They don't, for example, mean gay men, who they see as having cast their lot with special-pleading feminists and the nonmales that comprise the LGBT community.

One of the MRAs' ongoing gripes is the negative image of men put forward by the media—in films, adverts, sitcoms, and newspapers—where males are routinely portrayed as incompetent parents, useless husbands, or clumsy, immature, untidy morons (I should probably declare an interest here).

I'm all for moaning about stupid ads and witless sitcoms, but to attempt to dress this sort of thing up as discrimination—to say, "if they did it to women, all the feminists would be outraged"—is deeply misguided. An ad in which a male cyclist ogles a passing woman and then smashes into a postbox is not feminist propaganda, nor is it an example of violence against men.

Masculism and feminism aren't, of course, opposing sides of the same coin. They aren't even vaguely analogous. Feminists ask how we can tolerate a society where women still face discrimination and misogyny in the course of an ordinary working day. MRAs get exercised because girls are allowed to join the Scouts, but boys can't join the Girl Guides. Feminists seek solutions to problems that are concrete and specific (I'm being paid less than male colleagues; legislators wish to control my body). The tragedies befalling the modern masculist, meanwhile, remain woolly and impersonal (his traditional role is being usurped, or something). If, as a man, your biggest problem is your ongoing struggle to forge a positive gender identity in a changing world, then you don't have enough problems. If you need to be kept busy, you're welcome to some of mine.

None of this thinking featured in my attempt to

unpick the Sheilas' Wheels conundrum for my son. His nose for actuarial injustice notwithstanding, he would have been quite perplexed by the idea of misandry. It wasn't society's inbuilt bias against men that led to their paying higher insurance premiums in the first place (Sheilas' Wheels ain't no radical feminist collective; it's part of Esure). It was always just about the money.

He would not then, or now, accept that the goofy, postadolescent male characters who populate Judd Apatow films collectively constitute some sort of gender slur. When he sees a bumbling, incompetent dad in an oven cleaner advert, it doesn't hurt his feelings. When he compares Homer Simpson's "half-assed underparenting" with mine, he does not spy a feminist conspiracy—only eerie parallels.

I don't suppose I have ever inculcated my sons with anything better than my own personal brand of feminism (full support from someone who gracelessly accepts he's part of the problem), but I married a feminist with the same sort of foresight that led my mother to marry a dentist— she knew it would come in handy later on. If nothing else my sons will always know they have nothing to fear from feminism, that it's not feminism's fault that boys lag behind girls at school, or that there are loads more men than women in jail, or that men are involved in twice as many car accidents as women every year. If you are the son of a feminist, you can't really argue that feminism has held you back in any way. In fact, feminists are really the only people who discuss male issues with any solemnity. Men, by and large, keep quiet.

Whenever people seek to blame a specific group—immigrants, robots, feminists—for a difficulty that is transparently not their fault, it's usually because the problem in question is intractable, with varied and disputed causes and no obvious solution. But in many cases the big problems facing men are simple and eminently solvable. And the solutions lie with men.

We could improve male health statistics instantly, for example, if only men could be persuaded to go to the doctor more. Nobody really needs to be convinced of this. It's not a solution that requires any great innovation, or even intervention. All men have to do is, you know, change.

This is easier said than done, of course—ask women. Of course you should go to the doctor more—you know that—but I never go to the doctor, and I can't think of an argument that would persuade me to go, much less make you go. This is not me not telling you not to, by the way. You definitely should.

There are many things we could do to improve the lot of men, within and without marriage and family. My simple six-point plan is a bit brutal, and possibly a little anti-men, but I think it's a start:

Go to the doctor more. Try to think of looking after yourself as some kind of survival skill. Because that's precisely what it is.

Obey all safety guidelines issued by your workplace. Try to think of not getting injured as part of your job description.

Take steps to protect vulnerable men and boys. They are among the most overlooked people in society.

Seek common cause with feminists. They've done more to make the world a nicer place for men than men have.

Remember that men includes gay men. If we're going to stick up for our gender, let's not forget those at the actual chalk face of discrimination.

Avoid deploying casually sexist obscenities, even if you're using them on men, unless you really need to make a point in short order.

Stop driving like a dick.

When the new EU rules dictating gender-neutral insurance premiums came into force at the end of 2012, Sheilas' Wheels products were insulated from the worst impact of the inevitable price rises, ironically because most of its half a million car insurance customers were women (they've always offered car insurance to men—who knew?—but only fifty thousand of its main driver policy-holders were male). Under those circumstances it makes more sense to subsidize cheaper insurance for the men already on the books. Now that they can't charge them higher premiums, the only deterrent to men from signing up with Sheilas' Wheels is the name and the overwhelming use of pink on the website. It may well be enough.

I'm sure my son would have considered this outcome a victory for common sense, had he not by then turned eighteen and completely forgotten about his former outrage. But his innocent demand for fairness all those years ago seems to me to herald a future where men might fight their corner without rancor, without blaming feminism, without wasting time bemoaning the loss of some bygone notions of masculinity that were themselves imprisoning, and above all without the rank misogyny that taints, and frankly nullifies, much of the present debate.

20.

Subject to Change

I am, in so very many ways, not the man my wife married. To present just one small example: I am, at the time of writing, wearing a beard. Not a false one—it's attached.

For almost twenty years my wife knew me as a clean-shaven man. Well, not entirely; there have certainly been times in my life where I've lost the will to shave, mornings when I've looked in the bathroom mirror, razor in hand, and said to myself, "Have you got a bail hearing today? No? Then what are we doing here?"

But I always shaved for parties and photographs, and I never let it slide for more than a week, because I didn't want to end up with a beard. The beard, along with the hat and the bow tie, was for most of my lifetime filed under the generic style heading "NO." Beards, as far as I was concerned, were for lumberjacks and castaways. I couldn't conceive of a beard being a positive attribute. I had what I thought were strong, if ill-defined, objections to facial hair. Whenever I saw a man who appeared to be sporting some intentionally I would think: What could possibly be wrong with your face that's worse than a beard?

Then one day about two years ago, I grew one. I don't recall making an actual decision, but that's the great thing about a beard—it just happens by itself. It's the product of something you're not doing, the point where sloth meets affectation—the sweet spot I've been searching for my whole life.

Although it hardly counts as an achievement, the beard nevertheless became a talking point. "Hey, nice beard," friends would say, as if I'd knitted it. I really could not have done less to earn people's interest in me, or the subsequent polarization of opinion: I soon became aware of a section of the female population that doesn't like beards at all, but also of another section that will treat you as if you have a cute puppy strapped to your chin. I realized that I didn't know whether my wife fell into either of these categories. So taken was I with my new image—indeed, with having an image at all—that I forgot to consult the one person who mattered.

I was more than a month in when I finally said to my wife, "So, do you, um, like the beard?"

She appraised my face as if the question had not yet occurred to her—as if this were the first time she'd actually noticed anything was different.

"I don't mind the beard," she said. She looked at me again, as if perhaps she'd spoken too soon, but then she walked away without adding anything. And that was it—another odd change accommodated, folded into the marriage without protest or ceremony.

My wife is—in just as many ways—not the same woman I married. The woman I married claimed such a profound dislike of theater that I assumed she had a phobia about sharing an enclosed space with actors. I spent years trying to convince her she was wrong, but even when I was permitted to buy theater tickets she would invariably develop an illness on the day of the performance, and I would have to take one of the children. The thought of going actually made her sick.

Then, without warning, she changed her mind. She went to something and, to her surprise, she enjoyed it. She overcame her lifelong resistance to musicals. She started buying tickets for shows she'd read about. If I couldn't come, she'd go on her own. She went from phobic to aficionado, inside a year.

"I love a play, me," she says as we emerge from a seven-hour adaptation of *The Great Gatsby*, the one where they read the entire book out loud. This is a little irritating for the person who spent years sitting next to a child, but it's definitely an improvement: I can add it to a long list of things she has suddenly seen the point of after years of dismissiveness or hostility: shellfish, exercise, certain friends of mine, the Internet, etc.

It is perhaps the most unforeseen aspect of a

long marriage, this need to accommodate change —sometimes abrupt or remarkable change—in the other person. The best thing about marriage, at least initially, is that no change is required: someone is willing to marry you as you are, rubbish bits included. You don't have to fix anything—in fact you're under a bit of an obligation not to tinker. You can get richer or poorer, sicker or healthier, but you are meant to remain fundamentally you.

It doesn't quite work that way. You can know someone, but not for long. After twenty years of marriage even your cells will have been replaced several times over. Along the way opinions change, certainties erode, beliefs evaporate. Circumstances oblige us to become very different people in a relatively short space of time. At the beginning neither of you knows what kind of parent, or middle-aged person, the other will make. If you're lucky you both accede to full adulthood at roughly the same rate, in vaguely complementary ways.

Not all change in marriage can be hailed as progress, or even neutral adjustment. Sometimes people adopt unpleasant habits or objectionable political views. My wife has recently acquired a taste for the sort of rubbish reality television you find on MTV, and she's started playing Candy Crush on her phone in bed. The latter, in particular, drives me insane.

"Why?" she says. "Is it because you hate me being good at things?"

"No," I say. "It's because I'm tired, and there's a multisocket extension lead on my pillow."

"My phone needs charging, and the cord wouldn't reach."

I'll admit that I myself am not necessarily getting better every day in every way, and that many of my changes for the worse were unexpected. My wife couldn't have known when she met me that I would one day be nearly impossible to contact by e-mail, because there was no e-mail. How could I warn her? Back then I could never have envisaged a dystopian future where strangers could submit written questions to you while you were sitting alone in a room minding your own business.

She could not have predicted that I would develop a pathological hatred of the bread-slicing machine at Sainsbury's, that I would refuse to slice and bag our bread, even when specifically instructed to do so, and would instead make false claims about the machine being out of order.

"That's a lie," she says. "You just couldn't be arsed."

"I think there were some fingers stuck in it or something," I say. "No one wanted to talk about it."

Cumulatively these changes, both little and large, add up to two totally different people over the course of two decades. My wife is patently not the same woman I married, the woman who used to smoke but now chews nicotine gum, and who deposits the chewed pieces in the little well of the door handle of the driver's side of the car until it's practically overflowing with them, so that sometimes when she slams the door a few bounce out and land on the seat, and then the next person who drives sits on them unawares, and gets stuck there.

This disgusting and wholly unforeseen habit aside, to me she remains very like the girl I met in New York almost a quarter century ago, in that, from time to time, she still scares the shit out of me. That much, I think, will never change.

Conclusion

One day, midmarriage: I have a terrible assignment, and I hate it. In the service of an article I'm writing about life coaching, I've signed up with an Internet life coach, and he has e-mailed me some exercises to complete. For the first one I'm supposed to make a list of my qualities. Each statement must subscribe to the format "I am [quality]." The life coach wants a list of twenty qualities, but I'm not even sure I *have* twenty. The assignment is almost a week overdue, and the prospect of even beginning it makes me feel light-headed. I prefer to engage in introspection on my own terms.

At some point I decide it's worth trying to convert my problem into my wife's problem, because she has a knack for making the stupid and impossible seem stupid and simple. It's okay with the life coach—one is encouraged to enlist the aid of friends and family—but on this occasion it proves to be a mistake. My wife looks at the sheet of paper on which I have written nothing other than "MY QUALITIES," and a single, trailing, "I am . . ."

"Let's see," she says. "Helpful? No. Compassionate? No. Engaging? No. Sympathetic? No . . ."

"I see I've caught you in a peculiar mood," I say.

". . . Brave? No. Thoughtful? No. Enthusiastic? No . . ."

"Okay, thanks for your help," I say. "I can take it from here."

I leave the room thinking I should just write "I am married" and be done with it. The episode is not unlike one of our periodic unscheduled assessment evenings, when my wife suddenly decides to update my biographical index: Tim, the recent failings of; as bad parent; as emotional half-wit; laziness of; selfishness of; various undischarged obligations of. It is a condition of her gracious acceptance of my shortcomings as a husband and father that she is allowed to sit me down from time to time to tell me all about them.

When you become a husband there is no minimum requirement for competence; it is no surprise to me that I'm not terribly good at it, even after all this time. The bar was always set low, and insofar as it's been raised by cultural forces during my tenure, I have been content to limbo under it. Personally, I've always felt that being a good husband and father is a simple matter of occasionally reminding one's wife and children that they could do a whole lot worse.

"Seriously," I say. "Look around you." There is, of course, a bit of misdirection involved in pointing out that lots of families are saddled with terrible menfolk. I'm not only trying to draw their attention away from me, but also from all the husbands and fathers who are doing a much better job than I am—the fearless, the engaged, the charming, the well dressed. Forget about them, I'm saying. Concentrate on the deadbeats, and consider yourselves lucky.

Another assignment: in the middle of our first ever marriage counseling session, a recent episode from our lives is being scrutinized in some detail. The roof needed urgent repair, and my wife had to organize the entire project. I was, I freely admit in a spirit of full disclosure, no help at all. The counselor turns to my wife.

"What's it's like," he says, "for you to always have to be the adequate person?"

Ultimately, my experience of being a husband has been one of inadequacy, of not doing enough or being enough, and that having to suffice. It's often painful—by getting married I opened myself to a pretty comprehensive exploration of my capacity to disappoint. I could have easily arranged for myself a more solitary and insular life, where my deficiencies were less apparent, or obvious only to me. But the struggle to improve my performance, though rarely met with reward, is itself rewarding. Just like with DIY, I try not to let repeated failure get me down. To be an inadequate little man and still get up every morning and carry on—there's a kind of weird dignity in that.

My marriage is not, I would argue, a stereotypical tale of a hapless idiot rescued by a woman of great competence and extreme emotional literacy (though if you wish to read it that way, I can hardly object). The balance of capability may be tipped in my wife's favor, but like many pretty-successful-so-far marriages, ours is the product of a number of trade-offs. Occasionally there are instances when being married makes my life so much easier that it feels like I'm cheating, but this is just an aspect of the gear-like meshing of each other's strengths and weaknesses. One of us is outgoing and proactive; the other remembers what happened in the previous episode of *Breaking Bad*. One of us can't gut and scale a fish, and one of us can't be in the same room as an uncaged bird. I don't think it's important that you know which one is me.

Over twenty years ago I took a series of decisions, not all of them transparently wise, to which I have ascribed a single motivation: love. But if I'm honest, leaving my old life behind had, at that time, many unspoken attractions (it's not a bad idea to examine one's past for mercenary taint occasionally, since the fingerprints of self-interest can turn up all over the purest of intentions). Frankly, someone as timid and unhappy as I was then would have to be a fool to turn down a chance to reinvent himself at twenty-seven, to slip his moorings and sail off somewhere else, with love as his justification.

It was also easy, and the moment it got hard, I considered retreat. In those early days, when I found myself obliged to return to America for long periods whenever my tourist visa expired, my old life inevitably regained some of its former traction, the familiar tug of the path of least resistance. In dark moments I began to think about my future in terms of what wasn't meant to be. There were a few phone calls during which my English girlfriend expressed similar doubts, and suggested it might be better if I didn't come back.

"I just thought it was hopeless," she said when I asked her about it recently.

"What made you change your mind?" I said.

"What makes you think I've changed my mind?"

Fortunately for me (and her—let's not forget her), I didn't listen.

Ultimately I don't want to give love too much credit, if only because it was clear from the beginning that love alone would not be enough. Love may be the reason we embarked on the whole voyage in the first place, but the success of the expedition so far is, I think, down to another factor: we made a deal. Marriage is a bargain struck, and ours has held. Not bad for a contract that from the beginning contained the words "We can always get divorced."

There is, of course, still plenty of rough water ahead. Our children are nearly grown and poised to jump ship (like rats, if you will), a point in the journey where lots of previously well-navigated marriages seem to run aground. Our vessel may be a bit leaky (at this point I feel my tortuously extended marine metaphor could go two ways: if the "vessel" is the marriage, then the "leaks" are arguments, bouts of impatience, forgotten anniversaries, periods of alienation, cruel things said when drunk, etc.; if, however, the "vessel" is our house, then we're talking about actual water coming in through the cracks. Your choice), but it's all we have. I certainly don't want to be anywhere else. As far as I'm concerned, I'm aboard for the duration.

I mean it: lash me to the mast.

Acknowledgments

I would like to thank my friend and agent, Natasha Fairweather, and her American counterpart, Elyse Cheney, for supporting this book, and for their unending patience.

I am also deeply indebted to everyone at Blue Rider Press: David Rosenthal, Aileen Boyle, Phoebe Pickering, and Eliza Rosenberry. They were models of kindness and efficiency throughout, and also patient. Let's just say that everyone I mention from now on was also patient.

My UK editor, Clare Reihill, was a great source of encouragement and advice. My friend Martin Thomas, because he basically explained to me how this book should be structured while we were on a walk near his house, and also because he married the Miranda from page 32, thereby throwing my English girlfriend's living arrangements into disarray at a very opportune moment for me.

Seven of the Forty Guiding Principles of Gross Marital Happiness made their first appearance, in slightly different form, in an article in *Guardian Weekend* magazine from February 2013.

I owe many people at the *Guardian* thanks (including Merope Mills, Melissa Denes, Malik

Meer, Tim Lusher, Clare Margetson, Emily Wilson, and Rob Fearn), along with apologies for late copy, lame excuses, and letting my phone ring and ring.

My three sons, Barnaby, Johnnie, and Will, have been eerily understanding about my writing about them over the years. I stole their childhoods, and I gave them an Xbox 360 in return. That was the deal. Then I wrote a book and ruined Christmas. That wasn't part of the deal. I'm sorry.

Above all else I would like to thank my wife, not just for still being my wife (at the time of going to press), and for reading this book at various stages and being frank in her assessments, but for being someone to turn to during crises, panics, and other low moments. On at least four occasions I came to her wild-eyed and raw-voiced, moaning that the book was beyond me, its failure certain and giving up the only sane option. And each time she would look at me calmly and say, "I can't really deal with you when you're like this."

Sometimes a little impatience goes a long way.

About the Author

TIM DOWLING is an American journalist for the *Guardian*. He writes a weekly column for *Weekend* magazine. He lives with his wife and three sons in London.

Center Point Large Print
600 Brooks Road / PO Box 1
Thorndike, ME 04986-0001 USA

(207) 568-3717

US & Canada:
1 800 929-9108
www.centerpointlargeprint.com